Bhagavad-Gita
&
The Light Of Asia

Translations by

Edwin Arnold

Alight Publications

2016

Bhagavad-Gita & The Light of Asia

By Edwin Arnold

Published by Alight Publications in 2016

Alight Publications
PO Box 277
Live Oak, CA 95953

http://www.Alightbooks.com

Cover design © 2016 by Partap Singh. All rights reserved.

ISBN 1-931833-46-X

Printed in the United States of America

Dedicated
to the
Spiritual Pioneers
who have helped to
Illuminate Humanity

The Song Celestial.
or
Bhagavad-Gita
(From the Mahabharata)

**Being a Discourse Between Arjuna,
Prince of India, and the Supreme Being
Under the Form of Krishna**

**Translated from the Sanskrit Text
by
Sir Edwin Arnold,
M.A., K.C.I.E., C.S.I.**

1900

Dedication

TO INDIA

So have I read this wonderful and spirit-thrilling speech,
By Krishna and Prince Arjun held, discoursing each with each;
So have I writ its wisdom here,--its hidden mystery,
For England; O our India! as dear to me as She!

PREFACE

This famous and marvellous Sanskrit poem occurs as an episode of the Mahabharata, in the sixth--or "Bhishma"--Parva of the great Hindooepic. It enjoys immense popularity and authority in India, where it is reckoned as one of the ``Five Jewels,"--pancharatnani--of Devanagiri literature. In plain but noble language it unfolds a philosophical system which remains to this day the prevailing Brahmanic belief, blending as it does the doctrines of Kapila, Patanjali, and the Vedas. So lofty are many of its declarations, so sublime its aspirations, so pure and tender its piety, that Schlegel, after his study of the poem, breaks forth into this outburst of delight and praise towards its unknown author: "Magistrorum reverentia a Brachmanis inter sanctissima pietatis officia refertur. Ergo te primum, Vates sanctissime, Numinisque hypopheta! quisquis tandem inter mortales dictus tu fueris, carminis bujus auctor,, cujus oraculis mens ad excelsa quaeque,quaeque,, aeterna atque divina, cum inenarraoih quddam delectatione rapitur-te primum, inquam, salvere jubeo, et vestigia tua semper adore."

Lassen re-echoes this splendid tribute; and indeed, so striking are some of the moralities here inculcated, and so close the parallelism--oftimes actually verbal-- between its teachings and those of the New Testament, that a controversy has arisen between Pandits and Missionaries on the point whether the author borrowed from Christian sources, or the Evangelists and Apostles from him. This raises the question of its date, which cannot be positively settled. It must have been inlaid into the ancient epic at a period later tha that of the original Mahabharata, but Mr Kasinath Telang has offered some fair arguments to prove it anterior to the Christian era. The weight of evidence, however, tends to place its composition at about the third century after Christ; and perhaps there are really echoes in this Brahmanic poem of the lessons of Galilee, and of the Syrian incarnation.

Bhagavad Gita

Its scene is the level country between the Jumna and the Sarsooti rivers-now Kurnul and Jheend. Its simple plot consists of a dialogue held by Prince Arjuna, the brother of King Yudhisthira, with Krishna, the Supreme Deity, wearing the disguise of a charioteer. A great battle is impending between the armies of the Kauravas and Pandavas, and this conversation is maintained in a war-chariot drawn up between the opposing hosts.

The poem has been turned into French by Burnouf, into Latin by Lassen, into Italian by Stanislav Gatti, into Greek by Galanos, and into English by Mr. Thomson and Mr Davies, the prose transcript of the last-named being truly beyond praise for its fidelity and clearness. Mr Telang has also published at Bombay a version in colloquial rhythm, eminently learned and intelligent, but not conveying the dignity or grace of the original. If I venture to offer a translation of the wonderful poem after so many superior scholars, it is in grateful recognition of the help derived from their labours, and because English literature would certainly be incomplete without possessing in popular form a poetical and philosophical work so dear to India.

There is little else to say which the "Song Celestial" does not explain for itself. The Sanskrit original is written in the Anushtubh metre, which cannot be successfully reproduced for Western ears. I have therefore cast it into our flexible blank verse, changing into lyrical measures where the text itself similarly breaks. For the most part, I believe the sense to be faithfully preserved in the following pages; but Schlegel himself had to say: "In reconditioribus me semper poetafoster mentem recte divinasse affirmare non ausim." Those who would read more upon the philosophy of the poem may find an admirable introduction in the volume of Mr Davies, printed by Messrs Trubner & Co.

EDWIN ARNOLD, C.S.I.

CONTENTS

I. THE DISTRESS OF ARJUNA
II. THE BOOK OF DOCTRINES
III. VIRTUE IN WORK
IV. THE RELIGION OF KNOWLEDGE
V. RELIGION OF RENOUNCING WORKS
VI. RELIGION BY SELF-RESTRAINT
VII. RELIGION BY DISCERNMENT
VIII. RELIGION BY SERVICE OF THE SUPREME
IX. RELIGION BY THE KINGLY KNOWLEDGE AND THE KINGLY MYSTERY
X. RELIGION BY THE HEAVENLY PERFECTIONS
XI. THE MANIFESTING OF THE ONE AND MANIFOLD
XII. RELIGION OF FAITH
XIII. RELIGION BY SEPARATION OF MATTER AND SPIRIT
XIV. RELIGION BY SEPARATION FROM THE QUALITIES
XV. RELIGION BY ATTAINING THE SUPREME
XVI. THE SEPARATENESS OF THE DIVINE AND UNDVINE
XVII. RELIGION BY THE THREEFOLD FAITH
XVIII. RELIGION BY DELIVERANCE AND RENUNCIATION

Bhagavad Gita

CHAPTER I

Dhritirashtra:
Ranged thus for battle on the sacred plain--
On Kurukshetra--say, Sanjaya! say
What wrought my people, and the Pandavas?

Sanjaya:
When he beheld the host of Pandavas,
Raja Duryodhana to Drona drew,
And spake these words: "Ah, Guru! see this line,
How vast it is of Pandu fighting-men,
Embattled by the son of Drupada,
Thy scholar in the war! Therein stand ranked
Chiefs like Arjuna, like to Bhima chiefs,
Benders of bows; Virata, Yuyudhan,
Drupada, eminent upon his car,
Dhrishtaket, Chekitan, Kasi's stout lord,
Purujit, Kuntibhoj, and Saivya,
With Yudhamanyu, and Uttamauj
Subhadra's child; and Drupadi's;--all famed!
All mounted on their shining chariots!
On our side, too,--thou best of Brahmans! see
Excellent chiefs, commanders of my line,
Whose names I joy to count: thyself the first,
Then Bhishma, Karna, Kripa fierce in fight,
Vikarna, Aswatthaman; next to these
Strong Saumadatti, with full many more
Valiant and tried, ready this day to die
For me their king, each with his weapon grasped,
Each skilful in the field. Weakest-meseems-
Our battle shows where Bhishma holds command,
And Bhima, fronting him, something too strong!
Have care our captains nigh to Bhishma's ranks
Prepare what help they may! Now, blow my shell!"

Then, at the signal of the aged king,
With blare to wake the blood, rolling around
Like to a lion's roar, the trumpeter
Blew the great Conch; and, at the noise of it,
Trumpets and drums, cymbals and gongs and horns
Burst into sudden clamour; as the blasts
Of loosened tempest, such the tumult seemed!
Then might be seen, upon their car of gold
Yoked with white steeds, blowing their battle-shells,
Krishna the God, Arjuna at his side:
Krishna, with knotted locks, blew his great conch
Carved of the "Giant's bone;" Arjuna blew
Indra's loud gift; Bhima the terrible--
Wolf-bellied Bhima-blew a long reed-conch;
And Yudhisthira, Kunti's blameless son,
Winded a mighty shell, "Victory's Voice;"
And Nakula blew shrill upon his conch
Named the "Sweet-sounding," Sahadev on his
Called"Gem-bedecked," and Kasi's Prince on his.
Sikhandi on his car, Dhrishtadyumn,
Virata, Satyaki the Unsubdued,
Drupada, with his sons, (O Lord of Earth!)
Long-armed Subhadra's children, all blew loud,
So that the clangour shook their foemen's hearts,
With quaking earth and thundering heav'n.

Then 'twas-
Beholding Dhritirashtra's battle set,
Weapons unsheathing, bows drawn forth, the war
Instant to break-Arjun, whose ensign-badge
Was Hanuman the monkey, spake this thing
To Krishna the Divine, his charioteer:
"Drive, Dauntless One! to yonder open ground
Betwixt the armies; I would see more nigh
These who will fight with us, those we must slay
To-day, in war's arbitrament; for, sure,

Bhagavad Gita

On bloodshed all are bent who throng this plain,
   Obeying Dhritirashtra's sinful son."

Thus, by Arjuna prayed, (O Bharata!)
Between the hosts that heavenly Charioteer
Drove the bright car, reining its milk-white steeds
Where Bhishma led, and Drona, and their Lords.
"See!" spake he to Arjuna, "where they stand,
   Thy kindred of the Kurus:" and the Prince
Marked on each hand the kinsmen of his house,
Grandsires and sires, uncles and brothers and sons,
   Cousins and sons-in-law and nephews, mixed
With friends and honoured elders; some this side,
Some that side ranged: and, seeing those opposed,
   Such kith grown enemies-Arjuna's heart
   Melted with pity, while he uttered this:

Arjuna:
Krishna! as I behold, come here to shed
Their common blood, yon concourse of our kin,
My members fail, my tongue dries in my mouth,
   A shudder thrills my body, and my hair
Bristles with horror; from my weak hand slips
   Gandiv, the goodly bow; a fever burns
   My skin to parching; hardly may I stand;
The life within me seems to swim and faint;
   Nothing do I foresee save woe and wail!
   It is not good, O Keshav! nought of good
Can spring from mutual slaughter! Lo, I hate
   Triumph and domination, wealth and ease,
   Thus sadly won! Aho! what victory
Can bring delight, Govinda! what rich spoils
Could profit; what rule recompense; what span
Of life itself seem sweet, bought with such blood?
   Seeing that these stand here, ready to die,
For whose sake life was fair, and pleasure pleased,

And power grew precious:-grandsires, sires, and sons,
Brothers, and fathers-in-law, and sons-in-law,
Elders and friends! Shall I deal death on these
Even though they seek to slay us? Not one blow,
O Madhusudan! will I strike to gain

The rule of all Three Worlds; then, how much less
To seize an earthly kingdom! Killing these
Must breed but anguish, Krishna! If they be
Guilty, we shall grow guilty by their deaths;
Their sins will light on us, if we shall slay
Those sons of Dhritirashtra, and our kin;
What peace could come of that, O Madhava?
For if indeed, blinded by lust and wrath,
These cannot see, or will not see, the sin
Of kingly lines o'erthrown and kinsmen slain,
How should not we, who see, shun such a crime--
We who perceive the guilt and feel the shame--
O thou Delight of Men, Janardana?
By overthrow of houses perisheth
Their sweet continuous household piety,
And-rites neglected, piety extinct--
Enters impiety upon that home;
Its women grow unwomaned, whence there spring
Mad passions, and the mingling-up of castes,
Sending a Hell-ward road that family,
And whoso wrought its doom by wicked wrath.
Nay, and the souls of honoured ancestors
Fall from their place of peace, being bereft
Of funeral-cakes and the wan death-water.[FN#1]
So teach our holy hymns. Thus, if we slay
Kinsfolk and friends for love of earthly power,
Ahovat! what an evil fault it were!
Better I deem it, if my kinsmen strike,
To face them weaponless, and bare my breast
To shaft and spear, than answer blow with blow.

So speaking, in the face of those two hosts,
Arjuna sank upon his chariot-seat,
And let fall bow and arrows, sick at heart.

HERE ENDETH CHAPTER I. OF THE BHAGAVAD-GITA,
Entitled "Arjun-Vishad,"
Or "The Book of the Distress of Arjuna."

CHAPTER II

Sanjaya:
Him, filled with such compassion and such grief,
With eyes tear-dimmed, despondent, in stern words
The Driver, Madhusudan, thus addressed:

Krishna:
How hath this weakness taken thee? Whence springs
The inglorious trouble, shameful to the brave,
Barring the path of virtue? Nay, Arjun!
Forbid thyself to feebleness! it mars
Thy warrior-name! cast off the coward-fit!
Wake! Be thyself! Arise, Scourge of thy Foes!

Arjuna:
How can I, in the battle, shoot with shafts
On Bhishma, or on Drona-O thou Chief!--
Both worshipful, both honourable men?

Better to live on beggar's bread
With those we love alive,
Than taste their blood in rich feasts spread,
And guiltily survive!
Ah! were it worse-who knows?--to be
Victor or vanquished here,
When those confront us angrily
Whose death leaves living drear?
In pity lost, by doubtings tossed,
My thoughts-distracted-turn
To Thee, the Guide I reverence most,
That I may counsel learn:
I know not what would heal the grief
Burned into soul and sense,
If I were earth's unchallenged chief--
A god--and these gone thence!

Sanjaya:
So spake Arjuna to the Lord of Hearts,
And sighing,"I will not fight!" held silence then.
To whom, with tender smile, (O Bharata!)
While the Prince wept despairing 'twixt those hosts,
Krishna made answer in divinest verse:

Krishna:
Thou grievest where no grief should be! thou speak'st
Words lacking wisdom! for the wise in heart
Mourn not for those that live, nor those that die.
Nor I, nor thou, nor any one of these,
Ever was not, nor ever will not be,
For ever and for ever afterwards.
All, that doth live, lives always! To man's frame
As there come infancy and youth and age,
So come there raisings-up and layings-down
Of other and of other life-abodes,
Which the wise know, and fear not. This that irks--

Bhagavad Gita

Thy sense-life, thrilling to the elements--
Bringing thee heat and cold, sorrows and joys,
'Tis brief and mutable! Bear with it, Prince!
As the wise bear. The soul which is not moved,
The soul that with a strong and constant calm
Takes sorrow and takes joy indifferently,
Lives in the life undying! That which is
Can never cease to be; that which is not
Will not exist. To see this truth of both
Is theirs who part essence from accident,
Substance from shadow. Indestructible,
Learn thou! the Life is, spreading life through all;
It cannot anywhere, by any means,
Be anywise diminished, stayed, or changed.
But for these fleeting frames which it informs
With spirit deathless, endless, infinite,
They perish. Let them perish, Prince! and fight!
He who shall say, "Lo! I have slain a man!"
He who shall think, "Lo! I am slain!" those both
Know naught! Life cannot slay. Life is not slain!
Never the spirit was born; the spirit shall cease to be never;
Never was time it was not; End and Beginning are dreams!
Birthless and deathless and changeless
remaineth the spirit for ever;
Death hath not touched it at all, dead though the house of it seems!

Who knoweth it exhaustless, self-sustained,
Immortal, indestructible,--shall such
Say, "I have killed a man, or caused to kill?"

Nay, but as when one layeth
His worn-out robes away,
And taking new ones, sayeth,
"These will I wear to-day!"
So putteth by the spirit
Lightly its garb of flesh,

And passeth to inherit
A residence afresh.

I say to thee weapons reach not the Life;
Flame burns it not, waters cannot o'erwhelm,
Nor dry winds wither it. Impenetrable,
Unentered, unassailed, unharmed, untouched,
Immortal, all-arriving, stable, sure,
Invisible, ineffable, by word
And thought uncompassed, ever all itself,
Thus is the Soul declared! How wilt thou, then,--
Knowing it so,--grieve when thou shouldst not grieve?
How, if thou hearest that the man new-dead
Is, like the man new-born, still living man--
One same, existent Spirit--wilt thou weep?
The end of birth is death; the end of death
Is birth: this is ordained! and mournest thou,
Chief of the stalwart arm! for what befalls
Which could not otherwise befall? The birth
Of living things comes unperceived; the death
Comes unperceived; between them, beings perceive:
What is there sorrowful herein, dear Prince?

Wonderful, wistful, to contemplate!
Difficult, doubtful, to speak upon!
Strange and great for tongue to relate,
Mystical hearing for every one!
Nor wotteth man this, what a marvel it is,
When seeing, and saying, and hearing are done!

This Life within all living things, my Prince!
Hides beyond harm; scorn thou to suffer, then,
For that which cannot suffer. Do thy part!
Be mindful of thy name, and tremble not!
Nought better can betide a martial soul
Than lawful war; happy the warrior

Bhagavad Gita

To whom comes joy of battle--comes, as now,
Glorious and fair, unsought; opening for him
A gateway unto Heav'n. But, if thou shunn'st
This honourable field--a Kshattriya--
If, knowing thy duty and thy task, thou bidd'st
Duty and task go by--that shall be sin!
And those to come shall speak thee infamy
From age to age; but infamy is worse
For men of noble blood to bear than death!
The chiefs upon their battle-chariots
Will deem 'twas fear that drove thee from the fray.
Of those who held thee mighty-souled the scorn
Thou must abide, while all thine enemies
Will scatter bitter speech of thee, to mock
The valour which thou hadst; what fate could fall
More grievously than this? Either--being killed--
Thou wilt win Swarga's safety, or--alive
And victor--thou wilt reign an earthly king.
Therefore, arise, thou Son of Kunti! brace
Thine arm for conflict, nerve thy heart to meet--
As things alike to thee--pleasure or pain,
Profit or ruin, victory or defeat:
So minded, gird thee to the fight, for so
Thou shalt not sin!

Thus far I speak to thee
As from the "Sankhya"--unspiritually--
Hear now the deeper teaching of the Yog,
Which holding, understanding, thou shalt burst
Thy Karmabandh, the bondage of wrought deeds.
Here shall no end be hindered, no hope marred,
No loss be feared: faith--yea, a little faith--
Shall save thee from the anguish of thy dread.
Here, Glory of the Kurus! shines one rule--
One steadfast rule--while shifting souls have laws
Many and hard. Specious, but wrongful deem

The speech of those ill-taught ones who extol
The letter of their Vedas, saying, "This
Is all we have, or need;" being weak at heart
With wants, seekers of Heaven: which comes--they say--
As "fruit of good deeds done;" promising men
Much profit in new births for works of faith;
In various rites abounding; following whereon
Large merit shall accrue towards wealth and power;
Albeit, who wealth and power do most desire
Least fixity of soul have such, least hold
On heavenly meditation. Much these teach,
From Veds, concerning the "three qualities;"
But thou, be free of the "three qualities,"
Free of the "pairs of opposites,"*[FN#2]* and free
From that sad righteousness which calculates;
Self-ruled, Arjuna! simple, satisfied!*[FN#3]*
Look! like as when a tank pours water forth
To suit all needs, so do these Brahmans draw
Text for all wants from tank of Holy Writ.
But thou, want not! ask not! Find full reward
Of doing right in right! Let right deeds be
Thy motive, not the fruit which comes from them.
And live in action! Labour! Make thine acts
Thy piety, casting all self aside,
Contemning gain and merit; equable
In good or evil: equability
Is Yog, is piety!

Yet, the right act
Is less, far less, than the right-thinking mind.
Seek refuge in thy soul; have there thy heaven!
Scorn them that follow virtue for her gifts!
The mind of pure devotion--even here--
Casts equally aside good deeds and bad,
Passing above them. Unto pure devotion
Devote thyself: with perfect meditation

Bhagavad Gita

Comes perfect act, and the right-hearted rise--
More certainly because they seek no gain--
Forth from the bands of body, step by step,
To highest seats of bliss. When thy firm soul
Hath shaken off those tangled oracles
Which ignorantly guide, then shall it soar
To high neglect of what's denied or said,
This way or that way, in doctrinal writ.
Troubled no longer by the priestly lore,
Safe shall it live, and sure; steadfastly bent
On meditation. This is Yog--and Peace!

Arjuna:
What is his mark who hath that steadfast heart,
Confirmed in holy meditation? How
Know we his speech, Kesava? Sits he, moves he
Like other men?

Krishna:
When one, O Pritha's Son!
Abandoning desires which shake the mind--
Finds in his soul full comfort for his soul,
He hath attained the Yog--that man is such!
In sorrows not dejected, and in joys
Not overjoyed; dwelling outside the stress
Of passion, fear, and anger; fixed in calms
Of lofty contemplation;--such an one
Is Muni, is the Sage, the true Recluse!
He who to none and nowhere overbound
By ties of flesh, takes evil things and good
Neither desponding nor exulting, such
Bears wisdom's plainest mark! He who shall draw
As the wise tortoise draws its four feet safe
Under its shield, his five frail senses back
Under the spirit's buckler from the world
Which else assails them, such an one, my Prince!

Hath wisdom's mark! Things that solicit sense
Hold off from the self-governed; nay, it comes,
The appetites of him who lives beyond
Depart,--aroused no more. Yet may it chance,
O Son of Kunti! that a governed mind
Shall some time feel the sense-storms sweep, and wrest
Strong self-control by the roots. Let him regain
His kingdom! let him conquer this, and sit
On Me intent. That man alone is wise
Who keeps the mastery of himself! If one
Ponders on objects of the sense, there springs
Attraction; from attraction grows desire,
Desire flames to fierce passion, passion breeds
Recklessness; then the memory--all betrayed--
Lets noble purpose go, and saps the mind,
Till purpose, mind, and man are all undone.
But, if one deals with objects of the sense
Not loving and not hating, making them
Serve his free soul, which rests serenely lord,
Lo! such a man comes to tranquillity;
And out of that tranquillity shall rise
The end and healing of his earthly pains,
Since the will governed sets the soul at peace.
The soul of the ungoverned is not his,
Nor hath he knowledge of himself; which lacked,
How grows serenity? and, wanting that,
Whence shall he hope for happiness?

The mind
That gives itself to follow shows of sense
Seeth its helm of wisdom rent away,
And, like a ship in waves of whirlwind, drives
To wreck and death. Only with him, great Prince!
Whose senses are not swayed by things of sense--
Only with him who holds his mastery,
Shows wisdom perfect. What is midnight-gloom

To unenlightened souls shines wakeful day
To his clear gaze; what seems as wakeful day
Is known for night, thick night of ignorance,
To his true-seeing eyes. Such is the Saint!

And like the ocean, day by day receiving
Floods from all lands, which never overflows
Its boundary-line not leaping, and not leaving,
Fed by the rivers, but unswelled by those;--

So is the perfect one! to his soul's ocean
The world of sense pours streams of witchery;
They leave him as they find, without commotion,
Taking their tribute, but remaining sea.

Yea! whoso, shaking off the yoke of flesh
Lives lord, not servant, of his lusts; set free
From pride, from passion, from the sin of "Self,"
Toucheth tranquillity! O Pritha's Son!
That is the state of Brahm! There rests no dread
When that last step is reached! Live where he will,
Die when he may, such passeth from all 'plaining,
To blest Nirvana, with the Gods, attaining.

HERE ENDETH CHAPTER II. OF THE BHAGAVAD-GITA,
Entitled "Sankhya-Yog,"
Or "The Book of Doctrines."

CHAPTER III

Arjuna:
Thou whom all mortals praise, Janardana!
If meditation be a nobler thing
Than action, wherefore, then, great Kesava!
Dost thou impel me to this dreadful fight?
Now am I by thy doubtful speech disturbed!
Tell me one thing, and tell me certainly;
By what road shall I find the better end?

Krishna:
I told thee, blameless Lord! there be two paths
Shown to this world; two schools of wisdom.

First
The Sankhya's, which doth save in way of works
Prescribed[FN#4] by reason; next, the Yog, which bids
Attain by meditation, spiritually:
Yet these are one! No man shall 'scape from act
By shunning action; nay, and none shall come
By mere renouncements unto perfectness.
Nay, and no jot of time, at any time,
Rests any actionless; his nature's law
Compels him, even unwilling, into act;
[For thought is act in fancy]. He who sits
Suppressing all the instruments of flesh,
Yet in his idle heart thinking on them,
Plays the inept and guilty hypocrite:
But he who, with strong body serving mind,
Gives up his mortal powers to worthy work,
Not seeking gain, Arjuna! such an one
Is honourable. Do thine allotted task!
Work is more excellent than idleness;
The body's life proceeds not, lacking work.
There is a task of holiness to do,

Bhagavad Gita

Unlike world-binding toil, which bindeth not
The faithful soul; such earthly duty do
Free from desire, and thou shalt well perform
Thy heavenly purpose. Spake Prajapati--
In the beginning, when all men were made,
And, with mankind, the sacrifice-- "Do this!
Work! sacrifice! Increase and multiply
With sacrifice! This shall be Kamaduk,
Your 'Cow of Plenty,' giving back her milk
Of all abundance. Worship the gods thereby;
The gods shall yield thee grace. Those meats ye crave
The gods will grant to Labour, when it pays
Tithes in the altar-flame. But if one eats
Fruits of the earth, rendering to kindly Heaven
No gift of toil, that thief steals from his world."
Who eat of food after their sacrifice
Are quit of fault, but they that spread a feast
All for themselves, eat sin and drink of sin.
By food the living live; food comes of rain,
And rain comes by the pious sacrifice,
And sacrifice is paid with tithes of toil;
Thus action is of Brahma, who is One,
The Only, All-pervading; at all times
Present in sacrifice. He that abstains
To help the rolling wheels of this great world,
Glutting his idle sense, lives a lost life,
Shameful and vain. Existing for himself,
Self-concentrated, serving self alone,
No part hath he in aught; nothing achieved,
Nought wrought or unwrought toucheth him; no hope
Of help for all the living things of earth
Depends from him.[FN#5] Therefore, thy task prescribed
With spirit unattached gladly perform,
Since in performance of plain duty man
Mounts to his highest bliss. By works alone
Janak and ancient saints reached blessedness!

Moreover, for the upholding of thy kind,
Action thou should'st embrace. What the wise choose
The unwise people take; what best men do
The multitude will follow. Look on me,
Thou Son of Pritha! in the three wide worlds
I am not bound to any toil, no height
Awaits to scale, no gift remains to gain,
Yet I act here! and, if I acted not--
Earnest and watchful--those that look to me
For guidance, sinking back to sloth again
Because I slumbered, would decline from good,
And I should break earth's order and commit
Her offspring unto ruin, Bharata!
Even as the unknowing toil, wedded to sense,
So let the enlightened toil, sense-freed, but set
To bring the world deliverance, and its bliss;
Not sowing in those simple, busy hearts
Seed of despair. Yea! let each play his part
In all he finds to do, with unyoked soul.
All things are everywhere by Nature wrought
In interaction of the qualities.
The fool, cheated by self, thinks, "This I did"
And "That I wrought; "but--ah, thou strong-armed Prince!--
A better-lessoned mind, knowing the play
Of visible things within the world of sense,
And how the qualities must qualify,
Standeth aloof even from his acts. Th' untaught
Live mixed with them, knowing not Nature's way,
Of highest aims unwitting, slow and dull.
Those make thou not to stumble, having the light;
But all thy dues discharging, for My sake,
With meditation centred inwardly,
Seeking no profit, satisfied, serene,
Heedless of issue--fight! They who shall keep
My ordinance thus, the wise and willing hearts,
Have quittance from all issue of their acts;

Bhagavad Gita

But those who disregard My ordinance,
Thinking they know, know nought, and fall to loss,
Confused and foolish. 'Sooth, the instructed one
Doth of his kind, following what fits him most:
And lower creatures of their kind; in vain
Contending 'gainst the law. Needs must it be
The objects of the sense will stir the sense
To like and dislike, yet th' enlightened man
Yields not to these, knowing them enemies.
Finally, this is better, that one do
His own task as he may, even though he fail,
Than take tasks not his own, though they seem good.
To die performing duty is no ill;
But who seeks other roads shall wander still.

Arjuna:
Yet tell me, Teacher! by what force doth man
Go to his ill, unwilling; as if one
Pushed him that evil path?

Krishna:
Kama it is!
Passion it is! born of the Darknesses,
Which pusheth him. Mighty of appetite,
Sinful, and strong is this!--man's enemy!
As smoke blots the white fire, as clinging rust
Mars the bright mirror, as the womb surrounds
The babe unborn, so is the world of things
Foiled, soiled, enclosed in this desire of flesh.
The wise fall, caught in it; the unresting foe
It is of wisdom, wearing countless forms,
Fair but deceitful, subtle as a flame.
Sense, mind, and reason--these, O Kunti's Son!
Are booty for it; in its play with these
It maddens man, beguiling, blinding him.
Therefore, thou noblest child of Bharata!

Govern thy heart! Constrain th' entangled sense!
Resist the false, soft sinfulness which saps
Knowledge and judgment! Yea, the world is strong,
But what discerns it stronger, and the mind
Strongest; and high o'er all the ruling Soul.
Wherefore, perceiving Him who reigns supreme,
Put forth full force of Soul in thy own soul!
Fight! vanquish foes and doubts, dear Hero! slay
What haunts thee in fond shapes, and would betray!

HERE ENDETH CHAPTER III. OF THE BHAGAVAD-GITA,
Entitled "Karma-Yog,"
Or "The Book of Virtue in Work."

CHAPTER IV

Krishna:
This deathless Yoga, this deep union,
I taught Vivaswata,[FN#6] the Lord of Light;
Vivaswata to Manu gave it; he
To Ikshwaku; so passed it down the line
Of all my royal Rishis. Then, with years,
The truth grew dim and perished, noble Prince!
Now once again to thee it is declared--
This ancient lore, this mystery supreme--
Seeing I find thee votary and friend.

Arjuna:
Thy birth, dear Lord, was in these later days,
And bright Vivaswata's preceded time!
How shall I comprehend this thing thou sayest,
"From the beginning it was I who taught?"

Bhagavad Gita

Krishna:
Manifold the renewals of my birth
Have been, Arjuna! and of thy births, too!
But mine I know, and thine thou knowest not,
O Slayer of thy Foes! Albeit I be
Unborn, undying, indestructible,
The Lord of all things living; not the less--
By Maya, by my magic which I stamp
On floating Nature-forms, the primal vast--
I come, and go, and come. When Righteousness
Declines, O Bharata! when Wickedness
Is strong, I rise, from age to age, and take
Visible shape, and move a man with men,
Succouring the good, thrusting the evil back,
And setting Virtue on her seat again.
Who knows the truth touching my births on earth
And my divine work, when he quits the flesh
Puts on its load no more, falls no more down
To earthly birth: to Me he comes, dear Prince!
Many there be who come! from fear set free,
From anger, from desire; keeping their hearts
Fixed upon me--my Faithful--purified
By sacred flame of Knowledge. Such as these
Mix with my being. Whoso worship me,
Them I exalt; but all men everywhere
Shall fall into my path; albeit, those souls
Which seek reward for works, make sacrifice
Now, to the lower gods. I say to thee
Here have they their reward. But I am He
Made the Four Castes, and portioned them a place
After their qualities and gifts. Yea, I
Created, the Reposeful; I that live
Immortally, made all those mortal births:
For works soil not my essence, being works
Wrought uninvolved.[FN#7] Who knows me acting thus
Unchained by action, action binds not him;

And, so perceiving, all those saints of old
Worked, seeking for deliverance. Work thou
As, in the days gone by, thy fathers did.

Thou sayst, perplexed, It hath been asked before
By singers and by sages, "What is act,
And what inaction? "I will teach thee this,
And, knowing, thou shalt learn which work doth save
Needs must one rightly meditate those three--
Doing,--not doing,--and undoing. Here
Thorny and dark the path is! He who sees
How action may be rest, rest action--he
Is wisest 'mid his kind; he hath the truth!
He doeth well, acting or resting. Freed
In all his works from prickings of desire,
Burned clean in act by the white fire of truth,
The wise call that man wise; and such an one,
Renouncing fruit of deeds, always content.
Always self-satisfying, if he works,
Doth nothing that shall stain his separate soul,
Which--quit of fear and hope--subduing self--
Rejecting outward impulse--yielding up
To body's need nothing save body, dwells
Sinless amid all sin, with equal calm
Taking what may befall, by grief unmoved,
Unmoved by joy, unenvyingly; the same
In good and evil fortunes; nowise bound
By bond of deeds. Nay, but of such an one,
Whose crave is gone, whose soul is liberate,
Whose heart is set on truth--of such an one
What work he does is work of sacrifice,
Which passeth purely into ash and smoke
Consumed upon the altar! All's then God!
The sacrifice is Brahm, the ghee and grain
Are Brahm, the fire is Brahm, the flesh it eats
Is Brahm, and unto Brahm attaineth he

Bhagavad Gita

Who, in such office, meditates on Brahm.
Some votaries there be who serve the gods
With flesh and altar-smoke; but other some
Who, lighting subtler fires, make purer rite
With will of worship. Of the which be they
Who, in white flame of continence, consume
Joys of the sense, delights of eye and ear,
Forgoing tender speech and sound of song:
And they who, kindling fires with torch of Truth,
Burn on a hidden altar-stone the bliss
Of youth and love, renouncing happiness:
And they who lay for offering there their wealth,
Their penance, meditation, piety,
Their steadfast reading of the scrolls, their lore
Painfully gained with long austerities:
And they who, making silent sacrifice,
Draw in their breath to feed the flame of thought,
And breathe it forth to waft the heart on high,
Governing the ventage of each entering air
Lest one sigh pass which helpeth not the soul:
And they who, day by day denying needs,
Lay life itself upon the altar-flame,
Burning the body wan. Lo! all these keep
The rite of offering, as if they slew
Victims; and all thereby efface much sin.
Yea! and who feed on the immortal food
Left of such sacrifice, to Brahma pass,
To The Unending. But for him that makes
No sacrifice, he hath nor part nor lot
Even in the present world. How should he share
Another, O thou Glory of thy Line?

In sight of Brahma all these offerings
Are spread and are accepted! Comprehend
That all proceed by act; for knowing this,
Thou shalt be quit of doubt. The sacrifice

Which Knowledge pays is better than great gifts
Offered by wealth, since gifts' worth--O my Prince!
Lies in the mind which gives, the will that serves:
And these are gained by reverence, by strong search,
By humble heed of those who see the Truth
And teach it. Knowing Truth, thy heart no more
Will ache with error, for the Truth shall show
All things subdued to thee, as thou to Me.
Moreover, Son of Pandu! wert thou worst
Of all wrong-doers, this fair ship of Truth
Should bear thee safe and dry across the sea
Of thy transgressions. As the kindled flame
Feeds on the fuel till it sinks to ash,
So unto ash, Arjuna! unto nought
The flame of Knowledge wastes works' dross away!
There is no purifier like thereto
In all this world, and he who seeketh it
Shall find it--being grown perfect--in himself.
Believing, he receives it when the soul
Masters itself, and cleaves to Truth, and comes--
Possessing knowledge--to the higher peace,
The uttermost repose. But those untaught,
And those without full faith, and those who fear
Are shent; no peace is here or other where,
No hope, nor happiness for whoso doubts.
He that, being self-contained, hath vanquished doubt,
Disparting self from service, soul from works,
Enlightened and emancipate, my Prince!
Works fetter him no more! Cut then atwain
With sword of wisdom, Son of Bharata!
This doubt that binds thy heart-beats! cleave the bond
Born of thy ignorance! Be bold and wise!
Give thyself to the field with me! Arise!

HERE ENDETH CHAPTER IV. OF THE BHAGAVAD GITA,
"Jnana Yog,"Or "The Book of the Religion of Knowledge,"

CHAPTER V

Arjuna:
Yet, Krishna! at the one time thou dost laud
Surcease of works, and, at another time,
Service through work. Of these twain plainly tell
Which is the better way?

Krishna:
To cease from works
Is well, and to do works in holiness
Is well; and both conduct to bliss supreme;
But of these twain the better way is his
Who working piously refraineth not.

That is the true Renouncer, firm and fixed,
Who--seeking nought, rejecting nought--dwells proof
Against the "opposites."[FN#8] O valiant Prince!
In doing, such breaks lightly from all deed:
'Tis the new scholar talks as they were two,
This Sankhya and this Yoga: wise men know
Who husbands one plucks golden fruit of both!
The region of high rest which Sankhyans reach
Yogins attain. Who sees these twain as one
Sees with clear eyes! Yet such abstraction, Chief!
Is hard to win without much holiness.
Whoso is fixed in holiness, self-ruled,
Pure-hearted, lord of senses and of self,
Lost in the common life of all which lives--
A "Yogayukt"--he is a Saint who wends
Straightway to Brahm. Such an one is not touched
By taint of deeds. "Nought of myself I do!"
Thus will he think-who holds the truth of truths--
In seeing, hearing, touching, smelling; when
He eats, or goes, or breathes; slumbers or talks,
Holds fast or loosens, opes his eyes or shuts;

Always assured "This is the sense-world plays
With senses."He that acts in thought of Brahm,
Detaching end from act, with act content,
The world of sense can no more stain his soul
Than waters mar th' enamelled lotus-leaf.
With life, with heart, with mind,-nay, with the help
Of all five senses--letting selfhood go--
Yogins toil ever towards their souls' release.
Such votaries, renouncing fruit of deeds,
Gain endless peace: the unvowed, the passion-bound,
Seeking a fruit from works, are fastened down.
The embodied sage, withdrawn within his soul,
At every act sits godlike in "the town
Which hath nine gateways,"[FN#9] neither doing aught
Nor causing any deed. This world's Lord makes
Neither the work, nor passion for the work,
Nor lust for fruit of work; the man's own self
Pushes to these! The Master of this World
Takes on himself the good or evil deeds
Of no man--dwelling beyond! Mankind errs here
By folly, darkening knowledge. But, for whom
That darkness of the soul is chased by light,
Splendid and clear shines manifest the Truth
As if a Sun of Wisdom sprang to shed
Its beams of dawn. Him meditating still,
Him seeking, with Him blended, stayed on Him,
The souls illuminated take that road
Which hath no turning back--their sins flung off
By strength of faith. [Who will may have this Light;
Who hath it sees.] To him who wisely sees,
The Brahman with his scrolls and sanctities,
The cow, the elephant, the unclean dog,
The Outcast gorging dog's meat, are all one.

The world is overcome--aye! even here!
By such as fix their faith on Unity.

Bhagavad Gita

The sinless Brahma dwells in Unity,
And they in Brahma. Be not over-glad
Attaining joy, and be not over-sad
Encountering grief, but, stayed on Brahma, still
Constant let each abide! The sage whose sou
Holds off from outer contacts, in himself
Finds bliss; to Brahma joined by piety,
His spirit tastes eternal peace. The joys
Springing from sense-life are but quickening wombs
Which breed sure griefs: those joys begin and end!
The wise mind takes no pleasure, Kunti's Son!
In such as those! But if a man shall learn,
Even while he lives and bears his body's chain,
To master lust and anger, he is blest!
He is the Yukta; he hath happiness,
Contentment, light, within: his life is merged
In Brahma's life; he doth Nirvana touch!
Thus go the Rishis unto rest, who dwell
With sins effaced, with doubts at end, with hearts
Governed and calm. Glad in all good they live,
Nigh to the peace of God; and all those live
Who pass their days exempt from greed and wrath,
Subduing self and senses, knowing the Soul!

The Saint who shuts outside his placid soul
All touch of sense, letting no contact through;
Whose quiet eyes gaze straight from fixed brows,
Whose outward breath and inward breath are drawn
Equal and slow through nostrils still and close;
That one-with organs, heart, and mind constrained,
Bent on deliverance, having put away
Passion, and fear, and rage;--hath, even now,
Obtained deliverance, ever and ever freed.
Yea! for he knows Me Who am He that heeds
The sacrifice and worship, God revealed;
And He who heeds not, being Lord of Worlds,

Lover of all that lives, God unrevealed,
Wherein who will shall find surety and shield!

HERE ENDS CHAPTER V. OF THE BHAGAVAD-GITA,
Entitled "Karmasanyasayog,"
Or "The Book of Religion by Renouncing Fruit of Works."

CHAPTER VI

Krishna:
Therefore, who doeth work rightful to do,
Not seeking gain from work, that man, O Prince!
Is Sanyasi and Yogi--both in one
And he is neither who lights not the flame
Of sacrifice, nor setteth hand to task.
Regard as true Renouncer him that makes
Worship by work, for who renounceth not
Works not as Yogin. So is that well said:
"By works the votary doth rise to faith,
And saintship is the ceasing from all works;
Because the perfect Yogin acts--but acts
Unmoved by passions and unbound by deeds,
Setting result aside.

Let each man raise
The Self by Soul, not trample down his Self,
Since Soul that is Self's friend may grow Self's foe.
Soul is Self's friend when Self doth rule o'er Self,
But Self turns enemy if Soul's own self
Hates Self as not itself.[FN#10]

Bhagavad Gita

The sovereign soul
Of him who lives self-governed and at peace
Is centred in itself, taking alike
Pleasure and pain; heat, cold; glory and shame.
He is the Yogi, he is Yukta, glad
With joy of light and truth; dwelling apart
Upon a peak, with senses subjugate
Whereto the clod, the rock, the glistering gold
Show all as one. By this sign is he known
Being of equal grace to comrades, friends,
Chance-comers, strangers, lovers, enemies,
Aliens and kinsmen; loving all alike,
Evil or good.

Sequestered should he sit,
Steadfastly meditating, solitary,
His thoughts controlled, his passions laid away,
Quit of belongings. In a fair, still spot
Having his fixed abode,--not too much raised,
Nor yet too low,--let him abide, his goods
A cloth, a deerskin, and the Kusa-grass.
There, setting hard his mind upon The One,
Restraining heart and senses, silent, calm,
Let him accomplish Yoga, and achieve
Pureness of soul, holding immovable
Body and neck and head, his gaze absorbed
Upon his nose-end,[FN#11] rapt from all around,
Tranquil in spirit, free of fear, intent
Upon his Brahmacharya vow, devout,
Musing on Me, lost in the thought of Me.
That Yojin, so devoted, so controlled,
Comes to the peace beyond,--My peace, the peace
Of high Nirvana!

But for earthly needs
Religion is not his who too much fasts

Or too much feasts, nor his who sleeps away
An idle mind; nor his who wears to waste
His strength in vigils. Nay, Arjuna! call
That the true piety which most removes
Earth-aches and ills, where one is moderate
In eating and in resting, and in sport;
Measured in wish and act; sleeping betimes,
Waking betimes for duty.

When the man,
So living, centres on his soul the thought
Straitly restrained--untouched internally
By stress of sense--then is he Yukta. See!
Steadfast a lamp burns sheltered from the wind;
Such is the likeness of the Yogi's mind
Shut from sense-storms and burning bright to Heaven.
When mind broods placid, soothed with holy wont;
When Self contemplates self, and in itself
Hath comfort; when it knows the nameless joy
Beyond all scope of sense, revealed to soul--
Only to soul! and, knowing, wavers not,
True to the farther Truth; when, holding this,
It deems no other treasure comparable,
But, harboured there, cannot be stirred or shook
By any gravest grief, call that state "peace,"
That happy severance Yoga; call that man
The perfect Yogin!

Steadfastly the will
Must toil thereto, till efforts end in ease,
And thought has passed from thinking. Shaking off
All longings bred by dreams of fame and gain,
Shutting the doorways of the senses close
With watchful ward; so, step by step, it comes
To gift of peace assured and heart assuaged,
When the mind dwells self-wrapped, and the soul broods

Bhagavad Gita

Cumberless. But, as often as the heart
Breaks--wild and wavering--from control, so oft
Let him re-curb it, let him rein it back
To the soul's governance; for perfect bliss
Grows only in the bosom tranquillised,
The spirit passionless, purged from offence,
Vowed to the Infinite. He who thus vows
His soul to the Supreme Soul, quitting sin,
Passes unhindered to the endless bliss
Of unity with Brahma. He so vowed,
So blended, sees the Life-Soul resident
In all things living, and all living things
In that Life-Soul contained. And whoso thus
Discerneth Me in all, and all in Me,
I never let him go; nor looseneth he
Hold upon Me; but, dwell he where he may,
Whate'er his life, in Me he dwells and lives,
Because he knows and worships Me, Who dwell
In all which lives, and cleaves to Me in all.
Arjuna! if a man sees everywhere--
Taught by his own similitude--one Life,
One Essence in the Evil and the Good,
Hold him a Yogi, yea! well-perfected!

Arjuna:
Slayer of Madhu! yet again, this Yog,
This Peace, derived from equanimity,
Made known by thee--I see no fixity
Therein, no rest, because the heart of men
Is unfixed, Krishna! rash, tumultuous,
Wilful and strong. It were all one, I think,
To hold the wayward wind, as tame man's heart.

Krishna:
Hero long-armed! beyond denial, hard
Man's heart is to restrain, and wavering;

Yet may it grow restrained by habit, Prince!
By wont of self-command. This Yog, I say,
Cometh not lightly to th' ungoverned ones;
But he who will be master of himself
Shall win it, if he stoutly strive thereto.

Arjuna:
And what road goeth he who, having faith,
Fails, Krishna! in the striving; falling back
From holiness, missing the perfect rule?
Is he not lost, straying from Brahma's light,
Like the vain cloud, which floats 'twixt earth and heaven
When lightning splits it, and it vanisheth?
Fain would I hear thee answer me herein,
Since, Krishna! none save thou can clear the doubt.

Krishna:
He is not lost, thou Son of Pritha! No!
Nor earth, nor heaven is forfeit, even for him,
Because no heart that holds one right desire
Treadeth the road of loss! He who should fail,
Desiring righteousness, cometh at death
Unto the Region of the Just; dwells there
Measureless years, and being born anew,
Beginneth life again in some fair home
Amid the mild and happy. It may chance
He doth descend into a Yogin house
On Virtue's breast; but that is rare! Such birth
Is hard to be obtained on this earth, Chief!
So hath he back again what heights of heart
He did achieve, and so he strives anew
To perfectness, with better hope, dear Prince!
For by the old desire he is drawn on
Unwittingly; and only to desire
The purity of Yog is to pass
Beyond the Sabdabrahm, the spoken Ved.

But, being Yogi, striving strong and long,
Purged from transgressions, perfected by births
Following on births, he plants his feet at last
Upon the farther path. Such as one ranks
Above ascetics, higher than the wise,
Beyond achievers of vast deeds! Be thou
Yogi Arjuna! And of such believe,
Truest and best is he who worships Me
With inmost soul, stayed on My Mystery!

HERE ENDETH CHAPTER VI. OF THE BHAGAVAD-GITA,
Entitled "Atmasanyamayog,"
Or "The Book of Religion by Self-Restraint."

CHAPTER VII

Krishna:
Learn now, dear Prince! how, if thy soul be set
Ever on Me--still exercising Yog,
Still making Me thy Refuge--thou shalt come
Most surely unto perfect hold of Me.
I will declare to thee that utmost lore,
Whole and particular, which, when thou knowest,
Leaveth no more to know here in this world.

Of many thousand mortals, one, perchance,
Striveth for Truth; and of those few that strive--
Nay, and rise high--one only--here and there--
Knoweth Me, as I am, the very Truth.

Earth, water, flame, air, ether, life, and mind,
And individuality--those eight
Make up the showing of Me, Manifest.

These be my lower Nature; learn the higher,
Whereby, thou Valiant One! this Universe
Is, by its principle of life, produced;
Whereby the worlds of visible things are born
As from a Yoni. Know! I am that womb:
I make and I unmake this Universe:
Than me there is no other Master, Prince!
No other Maker! All these hang on me
As hangs a row of pearls upon its string.
I am the fresh taste of the water; I
The silver of the moon, the gold o' the sun,
The word of worship in the Veds, the thrill
That passeth in the ether, and the strength
Of man's shed seed. I am the good sweet smell
Of the moistened earth, I am the fire's red light,
The vital air moving in all which moves,
The holiness of hallowed souls, the root
Undying, whence hath sprung whatever is;
The wisdom of the wise, the intellect
Of the informed, the greatness of the great.
The splendour of the splendid. Kunti's Son!
These am I, free from passion and desire;
Yet am I right desire in all who yearn,
Chief of the Bharatas! for all those moods,
Soothfast, or passionate, or ignorant,
Which Nature frames, deduce from me; but all
Are merged in me--not I in them! The world--
Deceived by those three qualities of being--
Wotteth not Me Who am outside them all,
Above them all, Eternal! Hard it is
To pierce that veil divine of various shows
Which hideth Me; yet they who worship Me

Bhagavad Gita

Pierce it and pass beyond.

I am not known
To evil-doers, nor to foolish ones,
Nor to the base and churlish; nor to those
Whose mind is cheated by the show of things,
Nor those that take the way of Asuras.[FN#12]

Four sorts of mortals know me: he who weeps,
Arjuna! and the man who yearns to know;
And he who toils to help; and he who sits
Certain of me, enlightened.

Of these four,
O Prince of India! highest, nearest, best
That last is, the devout soul, wise, intent
Upon "The One." Dear, above all, am I
To him; and he is dearest unto me!
All four are good, and seek me; but mine own,
The true of heart, the faithful--stayed on me,
Taking me as their utmost blessedness,
They are not "mine,"but I--even I myself!
At end of many births to Me they come!
Yet hard the wise Mahatma is to find,
That man who sayeth, "All is Vasudev!"[FN#13]

There be those, too, whose knowledge, turned aside
By this desire or that, gives them to serve
Some lower gods, with various rites, constrained
By that which mouldeth them. Unto all such--
Worship what shrine they will, what shapes, in faith--
'Tis I who give them faith! I am content!
The heart thus asking favour from its God,
Darkened but ardent, hath the end it craves,
The lesser blessing--but 'tis I who give!
Yet soon is withered what small fruit they reap:

Those men of little minds, who worship so,
Go where they worship, passing with their gods.
But Mine come unto me! Blind are the eyes
Which deem th' Unmanifested manifest,
Not comprehending Me in my true Self!
Imperishable, viewless, undeclared,
Hidden behind my magic veil of shows,
I am not seen by all; I am not known--
Unborn and changeless--to the idle world.
But I, Arjuna! know all things which were,
And all which are, and all which are to be,
Albeit not one among them knoweth Me!

By passion for the "pairs of opposites,"
By those twain snares of Like and Dislike, Prince!
All creatures live bewildered, save some few
Who, quit of sins, holy in act, informed,
Freed from the "opposites,"and fixed in faith,
Cleave unto Me.

Who cleave, who seek in Me
Refuge from birth[FN#14] and death, those have the Truth!
Those know Me BRAHMA; know Me Soul of Souls,
The ADHYATMAN; know KARMA, my work;
Know I am ADHIBHUTA, Lord of Life,
And ADHIDAIVA, Lord of all the Gods,
And ADHIYAJNA, Lord of Sacrifice;
Worship Me well, with hearts of love and faith,
And find and hold me in the hour of death.

HERE ENDETH CHAPTER VII. OF THE BHAGAVAD-GITA,
Entitled "Vijnanayog,"
Or "The Book of Religion by Discernment."

Bhagavad Gita

CHAPTER VIII

Arjuna:
Who is that BRAHMA? What that Soul of Souls,
The ADHYATMAN? What, Thou Best of All!
Thy work, the KARMA? Tell me what it is
Thou namest ADHIBHUTA? What again
Means ADHIDAIVA? Yea, and how it comes
Thou canst be ADHIYAJNA in thy flesh?
Slayer of Madhu! Further, make me know
How good men find thee in the hour of death?

Krishna:
I BRAHMA am! the One Eternal GOD,
And ADHYATMAN is My Being's name,
The Soul of Souls! What goeth forth from Me,
Causing all life to live, is KARMA called:
And, Manifested in divided forms,
I am the ADHIBHUTA, Lord of Lives;
And ADHIDAIVA, Lord of all the Gods,
Because I am PURUSHA, who begets.
And ADHIYAJNA, Lord of Sacrifice,
I--speaking with thee in this body here--
Am, thou embodied one! (for all the shrines
Flame unto Me!) And, at the hour of death,
He that hath meditated Me alone,
In putting off his flesh, comes forth to Me,
Enters into My Being--doubt thou not!
But, if he meditated otherwise
At hour of death, in putting off the flesh,
He goes to what he looked for, Kunti's Son!
Because the Soul is fashioned to its like.

Have Me, then, in thy heart always! and fight!
Thou too, when heart and mind are fixed on Me,
Shalt surely come to Me! All come who cleave

With never-wavering will of firmest faith,
Owning none other Gods: all come to Me,
The Uttermost, Purusha, Holiest!

Whoso hath known Me, Lord of sage and singer,
Ancient of days; of all the Three Worlds Stay,
Boundless,--but unto every atom Bringer
Of that which quickens it: whoso, I say,

Hath known My form, which passeth mortal knowing;
Seen my effulgence--which no eye hath seen--
Than the sun's burning gold more brightly glowing,
Dispersing darkness,--unto him hath been

Right life! And, in the hour when life is ending,
With mind set fast and trustful piety,
Drawing still breath beneath calm brows unbending,
In happy peace that faithful one doth die,--

In glad peace passeth to Purusha's heaven.
The place which they who read the Vedas name
AKSHARAM, "Ultimate;" whereto have striven
Saints and ascetics--their road is the same.

That way--the highest way--goes he who shuts
The gates of all his senses, locks desire
Safe in his heart, centres the vital airs
Upon his parting thought, steadfastly set;
And, murmuring OM, the sacred syllable--
Emblem of BRAHM--dies, meditating Me.

For who, none other Gods regarding, looks
Ever to Me, easily am I gained
By such a Yogi; and, attaining Me,
They fall not--those Mahatmas--back to birth,
To life, which is the place of pain, which ends,

Bhagavad Gita

But take the way of utmost blessedness.

The worlds, Arjuna!--even Brahma's world--
Roll back again from Death to Life's unrest;
But they, O Kunti's Son! that reach to Me,
Taste birth no more. If ye know Brahma's Day
Which is a thousand Yugas; if ye know
The thousand Yugas making Brahma's Night,
Then know ye Day and Night as He doth know!
When that vast Dawn doth break, th' Invisible
Is brought anew into the Visible;
When that deep Night doth darken, all which is
Fades back again to Him Who sent it forth;
Yea! this vast company of living things--
Again and yet again produced--expires
At Brahma's Nightfall; and, at Brahma's Dawn,
Riseth, without its will, to life new-born.
But--higher, deeper, innermost--abides
Another Life, not like the life of sense,
Escaping sight, unchanging. This endures
When all created things have passed away:
This is that Life named the Unmanifest,
The Infinite! the All! the Uttermost.
Thither arriving none return. That Life
Is Mine, and I am there! And, Prince! by faith
Which wanders not, there is a way to come
Thither. I, the PURUSHA, I Who spread
The Universe around me--in Whom dwell
All living Things--may so be reached and seen!
. . . . *[FN#14]*

Richer than holy fruit on Vedas growing,
Greater than gifts, better than prayer or fast,

Such wisdom is! The Yogi, this way knowing,
Comes to the Utmost Perfect Peace at last.

HERE ENDETH CHAPTER VIII. OF THE BHAGAVAD-GITA,
Entitled "Aksharaparabrahmayog,"
Or "The book of Religion by Devotion to the One Supreme God."

CHAPTER IX

Krishna:
Now will I open unto thee--whose heart
Rejects not--that last lore, deepest-concealed,
That farthest secret of My Heavens and Earths,
Which but to know shall set thee free from ills,--
A royal lore! a Kingly mystery!
Yea! for the soul such light as purgeth it
From every sin; a light of holiness
With inmost splendour shining; plain to see;
Easy to walk by, inexhaustible!

They that receive not this, failing in faith
To grasp the greater wisdom, reach not Me,
Destroyer of thy foes! They sink anew
Into the realm of Flesh, where all things change!

By Me the whole vast Universe of things
Is spread abroad;--by Me, the Unmanifest!
In Me are all existences contained;
Not I in them!

Bhagavad Gita

Yet they are not contained,
Those visible things! Receive and strive to embrace
The mystery majestical! My Being--
Creating all, sustaining all--still dwells
Outside of all!

See! as the shoreless airs
Move in the measureless space, but are not space,
[And space were space without the moving airs];
So all things are in Me, but are not I.

At closing of each Kalpa, Indian Prince!
All things which be back to My Being come:
At the beginning of each Kalpa, all
Issue new-born from Me.

By Energy
And help of Prakriti my outer Self,
Again, and yet again, I make go forth
The realms of visible things--without their will--
All of them--by the power of Prakriti.

Yet these great makings, Prince! involve Me not
Enchain Me not! I sit apart from them,
Other, and Higher, and Free; nowise attached!

Thus doth the stuff of worlds, moulded by Me,
Bring forth all that which is, moving or still,
Living or lifeless! Thus the worlds go on!

The minds untaught mistake Me, veiled in form;--
Naught see they of My secret Presence, nought
Of My hid Nature, ruling all which lives.
Vain hopes pursuing, vain deeds doing; fed
On vainest knowledge, senselessly they seek
An evil way, the way of brutes and fiends.

But My Mahatmas, those of noble soul
Who tread the path celestial, worship Me
With hearts unwandering,--knowing Me the Source,
Th' Eternal Source, of Life. Unendingly
They glorify Me; seek Me; keep their vows
Of reverence and love, with changeless faith
Adoring Me. Yea, and those too adore,
Who, offering sacrifice of wakened hearts,
Have sense of one pervading Spirit's stress,
One Force in every place, though manifold!
I am the Sacrifice! I am the Prayer!
I am the Funeral-Cake set for the dead!
I am the healing herb! I am the ghee,
The Mantra, and the flame, and that which burns!
I am-of all this boundless Universe-
The Father, Mother, Ancestor, and Guard!
The end of Learning! That which purifies
In lustral water! I am OM! I am
Rig-Veda, Sama-Veda, Yajur-Ved;
The Way, the Fosterer, the Lord, the Judge,
The Witness; the Abode, the Refuge-House,
The Friend, the Fountain and the Sea of Life
Which sends, and swallows up; Treasure of Worlds
And Treasure-Chamber! Seed and Seed-Sower,
Whence endless harvests spring! Sun's heat is mine;
Heaven's rain is mine to grant or to withhold;
Death am I, and Immortal Life I am,
Arjuna! SAT and ASAT, Visible Life,
And Life Invisible!

Yea! those who learn
The threefold Veds, who drink the Soma-wine,
Purge sins, pay sacrifice--from Me they earn
Passage to Swarga; where the meats divine

Bhagavad Gita

Of great gods feed them in high Indra's heaven.
Yet they, when that prodigious joy is o'er,
Paradise spent, and wage for merits given,
Come to the world of death and change once more.

They had their recompense! they stored their treasure,
Following the threefold Scripture and its writ;
Who seeketh such gaineth the fleeting pleasure
Of joy which comes and goes! I grant them it!

But to those blessed ones who worship Me,
Turning not otherwhere, with minds set fast,
I bring assurance of full bliss beyond.

Nay, and of hearts which follow other gods
In simple faith, their prayers arise to me,
O Kunti's Son! though they pray wrongfully;
For I am the Receiver and the Lord
Of every sacrifice, which these know not
Rightfully; so they fall to earth again!
Who follow gods go to their gods; who vow
Their souls to Pitris go to Pitris; minds
To evil Bhuts given o'er sink to the Bhuts;
And whoso loveth Me cometh to Me.
Whoso shall offer Me in faith and love
A leaf, a flower, a fruit, water poured forth,
That offering I accept, lovingly made
With pious will. Whate'er thou doest, Prince!
Eating or sacrificing, giving gifts,
Praying or fasting, let it all be done
For Me, as Mine. So shalt thou free thyself
From Karmabandh, the chain which holdeth men
To good and evil issue, so shalt come
Safe unto Me-when thou art quit of flesh--
By faith and abdication joined to Me!

I am alike for all! I know not hate,
I know not favour! What is made is Mine!
But them that worship Me with love, I love;
They are in Me, and I in them!

Nay, Prince!
If one of evil life turn in his thought
Straightly to Me, count him amidst the good;
He hath the high way chosen; he shall grow
Righteous ere long; he shall attain that peace
Which changes not. Thou Prince of India!
Be certain none can perish, trusting Me!
O Pritha's Son! whoso will turn to Me,
Though they be born from the very womb of Sin,
Woman or man; sprung of the Vaisya caste
Or lowly disregarded Sudra,--all
Plant foot upon the highest path; how then
The holy Brahmans and My Royal Saints?
Ah! ye who into this ill world are come--
Fleeting and false--set your faith fast on Me!
Fix heart and thought on Me! Adore Me! Bring
Offerings to Me! Make Me prostrations! Make
Me your supremest joy! and, undivided,
Unto My rest your spirits shall be guided.

HERE ENDS CHAPTER IX. OF THE BHAGAVAD-GITA,
Entitled "Rajavidyarajaguhyayog,"
Or "The Book of Religion by the Kingly Knowledge and the
Kingly Mystery."

CHAPTER X

Krishna:[FN#16]
Hear farther yet, thou Long-Armed Lord! these latest words I say--
Uttered to bring thee bliss and peace, who lovest Me alway--
Not the great company of gods nor kingly Rishis know
My Nature, Who have made the gods and Rishis long ago;
He only knoweth-only he is free of sin, and wise,
Who seeth Me, Lord of the Worlds, with faith-enlightened eyes,
Unborn, undying, unbegun. Whatever Natures be
To mortal men distributed, those natures spring from Me!
Intellect, skill, enlightenment, endurance, self-control,
Truthfulness, equability, and grief or joy of soul,
And birth and death, and fearfulness, and fearlessness, and shame,
And honour, and sweet harmlessness,[FN#17]
and peace which is the same
Whate'er befalls, and mirth, and tears, and piety, and thrift,
And wish to give, and will to help,--all cometh of My gift!
The Seven Chief Saints, the Elders Four, the Lordly Manus set--
Sharing My work--to rule the worlds, these too did I beget;
And Rishis, Pitris, Manus, all, by one thought of My mind;
Thence did arise, to fill this world, the races of mankind;
Wherefrom who comprehends My Reign of mystic Majesty--
That truth of truths--is thenceforth linked in faultless faith to Me:
Yea! knowing Me the source of all, by Me all creatures wrought,
The wise in spirit cleave to Me, into My Being brought;
Hearts fixed on Me; breaths breathed to Me; praising Me,
each to each,
So have they happiness and peace, with pious thought and speech;
And unto these--thus serving well, thus loving ceaselessly--
I give a mind of perfect mood, whereby they draw to Me;
And, all for love of them, within their darkened souls I dwell,
And, with bright rays of wisdom's lamp, their ignorance dispel.

Arjuna:
Yes! Thou art Parabrahm! The High Abode!

The Great Purification! Thou art God
Eternal, All-creating, Holy, First,
Without beginning! Lord of Lords and Gods!
Declared by all the Saints--by Narada,
Vyasa Asita, and Devalas;
And here Thyself declaring unto me!
What Thou hast said now know I to be truth,
O Kesava! that neither gods nor men
Nor demons comprehend Thy mystery
Made manifest, Divinest! Thou Thyself
Thyself alone dost know, Maker Supreme!
Master of all the living! Lord of Gods!
King of the Universe! To Thee alone
Belongs to tell the heavenly excellence
Of those perfections wherewith Thou dost fill
These worlds of Thine; Pervading, Immanent!
How shall I learn, Supremest Mystery!
To know Thee, though I muse continually?
Under what form of Thine unnumbered forms
Mayst Thou be grasped? Ah! yet again recount,
Clear and complete, Thy great appearances,
The secrets of Thy Majesty and Might,
Thou High Delight of Men! Never enough
Can mine ears drink the Amrit[FN#18] of such words!

Krishna:
Hanta! So be it! Kuru Prince! I will to thee unfold
Some portions of My Majesty, whose powers are manifold!
I am the Spirit seated deep in every creature's heart;
From Me they come; by Me they live; at My word they depart!
Vishnu of the Adityas I am, those Lords of Light;
Maritchi of the Maruts, the Kings of Storm and Blight;
By day I gleam, the golden Sun of burning cloudless Noon;
By Night, amid the asterisms I glide, the dappled Moon!
Of Vedas I am Sama-Ved, of gods in Indra's Heaven
Vasava; of the faculties to living beings given

Bhagavad Gita

The mind which apprehends and thinks; of Rudras Sankara;
Of Yakshas and of Rakshasas, Vittesh; and Pavaka
Of Vasus, and of mountain-peaks Meru; Vrihaspati
Know Me 'mid planetary Powers; 'mid Warriors heavenly
Skanda; of all the water-floods the Sea which drinketh each,
And Bhrigu of the holy Saints, and OM of sacred speech;
Of prayers the prayer ye whisper;[FN#19] of hills Himala's snow,
And Aswattha, the fig-tree, of all the trees that grow;
Of the Devarshis, Narada; and Chitrarath of them
That sing in Heaven, and Kapila of Munis, and the gem
Of flying steeds, Uchchaisravas, from Amrit-wave which burst;
Of elephants Airavata; of males the Best and First;
Of weapons Heav'n's hot thunderbolt; of cows white Kamadhuk,
From whose great milky udder-teats all hearts' desires are strook;
Vasuki of the serpent-tribes, round Mandara entwined;
And thousand-fanged Ananta, on whose broad coils reclined
Leans Vishnu; and of water-things Varuna; Aryam
Of Pitris, and, of those that judge, Yama the Judge I am;
Of Daityas dread Prahlada; of what metes days and years,
Time's self I am; of woodland-beasts-buffaloes, deers, and bears-
The lordly-painted tiger; of birds the vast Garud,
The whirlwind 'mid the winds; 'mid chiefs Rama with
blood imbrued,
Makar 'mid fishes of the sea, and Ganges 'mid the streams;
Yea! First, and Last, and Centre of all which is or seems
I am, Arjuna! Wisdom Supreme of what is wise,
Words on the uttering lips I am, and eyesight of the eyes,
And "A" of written characters, Dwandwa[FN#20]
of knitted speech,
And Endless Life, and boundless Love, whose power
sustaineth each;
And bitter Death which seizes all, and joyous sudden Birth,
Which brings to light all beings that are to be on earth;
And of the viewless virtues, Fame, Fortune, Song am I,
And Memory, and Patience; and Craft, and Constancy:
Of Vedic hymns the Vrihatsam, of metres Gayatri,

Of months the Margasirsha, of all the seasons three
The flower-wreathed Spring; in dicer's-play the conquering
Double-Eight;
The splendour of the splendid, and the greatness of the great,
Victory I am, and Action! and the goodness of the good,
And Vasudev of Vrishni's race, and of this Pandu brood
Thyself!--Yea, my Arjuna! thyself; for thou art Mine!
Of poets Usana, of saints Vyasa, sage divine;
The policy of conquerors, the potency of kings,
The great unbroken silence in learning's secret things;
The lore of all the learned, the seed of all which springs.
Living or lifeless, still or stirred, whatever beings be,
None of them is in all the worlds, but it exists by Me!
Nor tongue can tell, Arjuna! nor end of telling come
Of these My boundless glories, whereof I teach thee some;
For wheresoe'er is wondrous work, and majesty, and might,
From Me hath all proceeded. Receive thou this aright!
Yet how shouldst thou receive, O Prince! the vastness of this word?
I, who am all, and made it all, abide its separate Lord!

HERE ENDETH CHAPTER X. OF THE BHAGAVAD-GITA,
Entitled "Vibhuti Yog,"
Or "The Book of Religion by the Heavenly Perfections."

CHAPTER XI

Arjuna:
This, for my soul's peace, have I heard from Thee,
The unfolding of the Mystery Supreme
Named Adhyatman; comprehending which,

Bhagavad Gita

My darkness is dispelled; for now I know--
O Lotus-eyed![*FN#21*]--whence is the birth of men,
And whence their death, and what the majesties
Of Thine immortal rule. Fain would I see,
As thou Thyself declar'st it, Sovereign Lord!
The likeness of that glory of Thy Form
Wholly revealed. O Thou Divinest One!
If this can be, if I may bear the sight,
Make Thyself visible, Lord of all prayers!
Show me Thy very self, the Eternal God!

Krishna:
Gaze, then, thou Son of Pritha! I manifest for thee
Those hundred thousand thousand shapes that clothe my Mystery:
I show thee all my semblances, infinite, rich, divine,
My changeful hues, my countless forms. See! in this face of mine,
Adityas, Vasus, Rudras, Aswins, and Maruts; see
Wonders unnumbered, Indian Prince! revealed to none save thee.
Behold! this is the Universe!--Look! what is live and dead
I gather all in one--in Me! Gaze, as thy lips have said,
On GOD ETERNAL, VERY GOD! See Me! see what
thou prayest!

Thou canst not!--nor, with human eyes, Arjuna! ever mayest!
Therefore I give thee sense divine. Have other eyes, new light!
And, look! This is My glory, unveiled to mortal sight!

Sanjaya:
Then, O King! the God, so saying,
Stood, to Pritha's Son displaying
All the splendour, wonder, dread
Of His vast Almighty-head.
Out of countless eyes beholding,
Out of countless mouths commanding,
Countless mystic forms enfolding
In one Form: supremely standing

Countless radiant glories wearing,
Countless heavenly weapons bearing,
Crowned with garlands of star-clusters,
Robed in garb of woven lustres,
Breathing from His perfect Presence
Breaths of every subtle essence
Of all heavenly odours; shedding
Blinding brilliance; overspreading--
Boundless, beautiful--all spaces
With His all-regarding faces;
So He showed! If there should rise
Suddenly within the skies
Sunburst of a thousand suns
Flooding earth with beams undeemed-of,
Then might be that Holy One's
Majesty and radiance dreamed of!

So did Pandu's Son behold
All this universe enfold
All its huge diversity
Into one vast shape, and be
Visible, and viewed, and blended
In one Body--subtle, splendid,
Nameless--th' All-comprehending
God of Gods, the Never-Ending
Deity!

But, sore amazed,
Thrilled, o'erfilled, dazzled, and dazed,
Arjuna knelt; and bowed his head,
And clasped his palms; and cried, and said:

Arjuna:
Yea! I have seen! I see!
Lord! all is wrapped in Thee!
The gods are in Thy glorious frame! the creatures

Bhagavad Gita

Of earth, and heaven, and hell
In Thy Divine form dwell,
And in Thy countenance shine all the features

Of Brahma, sitting lone
Upon His lotus-throne;
Of saints and sages, and the serpent races
Ananta, Vasuki;
Yea! mightiest Lord! I see
Thy thousand thousand arms, and breasts, and faces,
And eyes,--on every side
Perfect, diversified;
And nowhere end of Thee, nowhere beginning,
Nowhere a centre! Shifts--
Wherever soul's gaze lifts--
Thy central Self, all-wielding, and all-winning!

Infinite King! I see
The anadem on Thee,
The club, the shell, the discus; see Thee burning
In beams insufferable,
Lighting earth, heaven, and hell
With brilliance blazing, glowing, flashing; turning

Darkness to dazzling day,
Look I whichever way;
Ah, Lord! I worship Thee, the Undivided,
The Uttermost of thought,
The Treasure-Palace wrought
To hold the wealth of the worlds; the Shield provided

To shelter Virtue's laws;
The Fount whence Life's stream draws
All waters of all rivers of all being:
The One Unborn, Unending:
Unchanging and Unblending!

With might and majesty, past thought, past seeing!

    Silver of moon and gold
    Of sun are glories rolled
From Thy great eyes; Thy visage, beaming tender
    Throughout the stars and skies,
    Doth to warm life surprise
Thy Universe. The worlds are filled with wonder

    Of Thy perfections! Space
    Star-sprinkled, and void place
From pole to pole of the Blue, from bound to bound,
    Hath Thee in every spot,
    Thee, Thee!--Where Thou art not,
O Holy, Marvellous Form! is nowhere found!

    O Mystic, Awful One!
    At sight of Thee, made known,
The Three Worlds quake; the lower gods draw nigh Thee;
    They fold their palms, and bow
    Body, and breast, and brow,
And, whispering worship, laud and magnify Thee!

    Rishis and Siddhas cry
    "Hail! Highest Majesty!"
From sage and singer breaks the hymn of glory
    In dulcet harmony,
    Sounding the praise of Thee;
While countless companies take up the story,

    Rudras, who ride the storms,
    Th' Adityas' shining forms,
Vasus and Sadhyas, Viswas, Ushmapas;
    Maruts, and those great Twins
    The heavenly, fair, Aswins,
Gandharvas, Rakshasas, Siddhas, and Asuras,[FN#22]--

Bhagavad Gita

These see Thee, and revere
In sudden-stricken fear;
Yea! the Worlds,--seeing Thee with form stupendous,
With faces manifold,
With eyes which all behold,
Unnumbered eyes, vast arms, members tremendous,

Flanks, lit with sun and star,
Feet planted near and far,
Tushes of terror, mouths wrathful and tender;--
The Three wide Worlds before Thee
Adore, as I adore Thee,
Quake, as I quake, to witness so much splendour!

I mark Thee strike the skies
With front, in wondrous wise
Huge, rainbow-painted, glittering; and thy mouth
Opened, and orbs which see
All things, whatever be
In all Thy worlds, east, west, and north and south.

O Eyes of God! O Head!
My strength of soul is fled,
Gone is heart's force, rebuked is mind's desire!
When I behold Thee so,
With awful brows a-glow,
With burning glance, and lips lighted by fire

Fierce as those flames which shall
Consume, at close of all,
Earth, Heaven! Ah me! I see no Earth and Heaven!
Thee, Lord of Lords! I see,
Thee only-only Thee!
Now let Thy mercy unto me be given,

Thou Refuge of the World!

Lo! to the cavern hurled
Of Thy wide-opened throat, and lips white-tushed,
I see our noblest ones,
Great Dhritarashtra's sons,
Bhishma, Drona, and Karna, caught and crushed!

The Kings and Chiefs drawn in,
That gaping gorge within;
The best of both these armies torn and riven!
Between Thy jaws they lie
Mangled full bloodily,
Ground into dust and death! Like streams down-driven

With helpless haste, which go
In headlong furious flow
Straight to the gulfing deeps of th' unfilled ocean,
So to that flaming cave
Those heroes great and brave
Pour, in unending streams, with helpless motion!

Like moths which in the night
Flutter towards a light,
Drawn to their fiery doom, flying and dying,
So to their death still throng,
Blind, dazzled, borne along
Ceaselessly, all those multitudes, wild flying!

Thou, that hast fashioned men,
Devourest them again,
One with another, great and small, alike!
The creatures whom Thou mak'st,
With flaming jaws Thou tak'st,
Lapping them up! Lord God! Thy terrors strike

From end to end of earth,
Filling life full, from birth

Bhagavad Gita

To death, with deadly, burning, lurid dread!
Ah, Vishnu! make me know
Why is Thy visage so?
Who art Thou, feasting thus upon Thy dead?
Who? awful Deity!
I bow myself to Thee,
Namostu Te, Devavara! Prasid![*FN#23*]
O Mightiest Lord! rehearse
Why hast Thou face so fierce?
Whence doth this aspect horrible proceed?

Krishna:
Thou seest Me as Time who kills,
Time who brings all to doom,
The Slayer Time, Ancient of Days, come hither to consume;
Excepting thee, of all these hosts of hostile chiefs arrayed,
There stands not one shall leave alive the battlefield! Dismayed
No longer be! Arise! obtain renown! destroy thy foes!
Fight for the kingdom waiting thee when thou hast
vanquished those.
By Me they fall--not thee! the stroke of death is dealt them now,
Even as they show thus gallantly; My instrument art thou!
Strike, strong-armed Prince, at Drona! at Bhishma strike!
deal death
On Karna, Jyadratha; stay all their warlike breath!
'Tis I who bid them perish! Thou wilt but slay the slain;
Fight! they must fall, and thou must live, victor upon this plain!

Sanjaya:
Hearing mighty Keshav's word,
Tremblingly that helmed Lord
Clasped his lifted palms, and--praying
Grace of Krishna--stood there, saying,
With bowed brow and accents broken,
These words, timorously spoken:

Arjuna:
Worthily, Lord of Might!
The whole world hath delight
In Thy surpassing power, obeying Thee;
The Rakshasas, in dread
At sight of Thee, are sped
To all four quarters; and the company

Of Siddhas sound Thy name.
How should they not proclaim
Thy Majesties, Divinest, Mightiest?
Thou Brahm, than Brahma greater!
Thou Infinite Creator!
Thou God of gods, Life's Dwelling-place and Rest!

Thou, of all souls the Soul!
The Comprehending Whole!
Of being formed, and formless being the Framer;
O Utmost One! O Lord!
Older than eld, Who stored
The worlds with wealth of life! O Treasure-Claimer,

Who wottest all, and art
Wisdom Thyself! O Part
In all, and All; for all from Thee have risen
Numberless now I see
The aspects are of Thee!
Vayu[FN#24] Thou art, and He who keeps the prison

Of Narak, Yama dark;
And Agni's shining spark;
Varuna's waves are Thy waves. Moon and starlight
Are Thine! Prajapati
Art Thou, and 'tis to Thee
They knelt in worshipping the old world's far light,

Bhagavad Gita

The first of mortal men.
Again, Thou God! again
A thousand thousand times be magnified!
Honour and worship be--
Glory and praise,--to Thee
Namo, Namaste, cried on every side;

Cried here, above, below,
Uttered when Thou dost go,
Uttered where Thou dost come! Namo! we call;
Namostu! God adored!
Namostu! Nameless Lord!
Hail to Thee! Praise to Thee! Thou One in all;

For Thou art All! Yea, Thou!
Ah! if in anger now
Thou shouldst remember I did think Thee Friend,
Speaking with easy speech,
As men use each to each;
Did call Thee "Krishna," "Prince," nor comprehend

Thy hidden majesty,
The might, the awe of Thee;
Did, in my heedlessness, or in my love,
On journey, or in jest,
Or when we lay at rest,
Sitting at council, straying in the grove,

Alone, or in the throng,
Do Thee, most Holy! wrong,
Be Thy grace granted for that witless sin!
For Thou art, now I know,
Father of all below,
Of all above, of all the worlds within

Guru of Gurus; more

To reverence and adore
Than all which is adorable and high!
How, in the wide worlds three
Should any equal be?
Should any other share Thy Majesty?

Therefore, with body bent
And reverent intent,
I praise, and serve, and seek Thee, asking grace.
As father to a son,
As friend to friend, as one
Who loveth to his lover, turn Thy face

In gentleness on me!
Good is it I did see
This unknown marvel of Thy Form! But fear
Mingles with joy! Retake,
Dear Lord! for pity's sake
Thine earthly shape, which earthly eyes may bear!

Be merciful, and show
The visage that I know;
Let me regard Thee, as of yore, arrayed
With disc and forehead-gem,
With mace and anadem,
Thou that sustainest all things! Undismayed

Let me once more behold
The form I loved of old,
Thou of the thousand arms and countless eyes!
This frightened heart is fain
To see restored again
My Charioteer, in Krishna's kind disguise.

Krishna:
Yea! thou hast seen, Arjuna! because I loved thee well,

Bhagavad Gita

The secret countenance of Me, revealed by mystic spell,
Shining, and wonderful, and vast, majestic, manifold,
Which none save thou in all the years had favour to behold;
For not by Vedas cometh this, nor sacrifice, nor alms,
Nor works well-done, nor penance long, nor prayers,
nor chaunted psalms,
That mortal eyes should bear to view the Immortal Soul unclad,
Prince of the Kurus! This was kept for thee alone! Be glad!
Let no more trouble shake thy heart, because thine eyes have seen
My terror with My glory. As I before have been
So will I be again for thee; with lightened heart behold!
Once more I am thy Krishna, the form thou knew'st of old!

Sanjaya:
These words to Arjuna spake
Vasudev, and straight did take
Back again the semblance dear
Of the well-loved charioteer;
Peace and joy it did restore
When the Prince beheld once more
Mighty BRAHMA's form and face
Clothed in Krishna's gentle grace.

Arjuna:
Now that I see come back, Janardana!
This friendly human frame, my mind can think
Calm thoughts once more; my heart beats still again!

Krishna:
Yea! it was wonderful and terrible
To view me as thou didst, dear Prince! The gods
Dread and desire continually to view!
Yet not by Vedas, nor from sacrifice,
Nor penance, nor gift-giving, nor with prayer
Shall any so behold, as thou hast seen!
Only by fullest service, perfect faith,

And uttermost surrender am I known
And seen, and entered into, Indian Prince!
Who doeth all for Me; who findeth Me
In all; adoreth always; loveth all
Which I have made, and Me, for Love's sole end
That man, Arjuna! unto Me doth wend.

HERE ENDETH CHAPTER XI. OF THE BHAGAVAD-GITA,
Entitled "Viswarupadarsanam,"
Or "The Book of the Manifesting of the One and Manifold."

CHAPTER XII

Arjuna:
Lord! of the men who serve Thee--true in heart--
As God revealed; and of the men who serve,
Worshipping Thee Unrevealed, Unbodied, Far,
Which take the better way of faith and life?

Krishna:
Whoever serve Me--as I show Myself--
Constantly true, in full devotion fixed,
Those hold I very holy. But who serve--
Worshipping Me The One, The Invisible,
The Unrevealed, Unnamed, Unthinkable,
Uttermost, All-pervading, Highest, Sure--
Who thus adore Me, mastering their sense,
Of one set mind to all, glad in all good,
These blessed souls come unto Me.

Bhagavad Gita

Yet, hard
The travail is for such as bend their minds
To reach th' Unmanifest That viewless path
Shall scarce be trod by man bearing the flesh!
But whereso any doeth all his deeds
Renouncing self for Me, full of Me, fixed
To serve only the Highest, night and day
Musing on Me--him will I swiftly lift
Forth from life's ocean of distress and death,
Whose soul clings fast to Me. Cling thou to Me!
Clasp Me with heart and mind! so shalt thou dwell
Surely with Me on high. But if thy thought
Droops from such height; if thou be'st weak to set
Body and soul upon Me constantly,
Despair not! give Me lower service! seek
To reach Me, worshipping with steadfast will;
And, if thou canst not worship steadfastly,
Work for Me, toil in works pleasing to Me!
For he that laboureth right for love of Me
Shall finally attain! But, if in this
Thy faint heart fails, bring Me thy failure! find
Refuge in Me! let fruits of labour go,
Renouncing hope for Me, with lowliest heart,
So shalt thou come; for, though to know is more
Than diligence, yet worship better is
Than knowing, and renouncing better still.
Near to renunciation--very near--
Dwelleth Eternal Peace!

Who hateth nought
Of all which lives, living himself benign,
Compassionate, from arrogance exempt,
Exempt from love of self, unchangeable
By good or ill; patient, contented, firm
In faith, mastering himself, true to his word,
Seeking Me, heart and soul; vowed unto Me,--

That man I love! Who troubleth not his kind,
And is not troubled by them; clear of wrath,
Living too high for gladness, grief, or fear,
That man I love! Who, dwelling quiet-eyed,[FN#25]
Stainless, serene, well-balanced, unperplexed,
Working with Me, yet from all works detached,
That man I love! Who, fixed in faith on Me,
Dotes upon none, scorns none; rejoices not,
And grieves not, letting good or evil hap
Light when it will, and when it will depart,
That man I love! Who, unto friend and foe
Keeping an equal heart, with equal mind
Bears shame and glory; with an equal peace
Takes heat and cold, pleasure and pain; abides
Quit of desires, hears praise or calumny
In passionless restraint, unmoved by each;
Linked by no ties to earth, steadfast in Me,
That man I love! But most of all I love
Those happy ones to whom 'tis life to live
In single fervid faith and love unseeing,
Drinking the blessed Amrit of my Being!

HERE ENDETH CHAPTER XII. OF THE BHAGAVAD-GITA,
Entitled "Bhaktiyog,"
Or"The Book of the Religion of Faith."

Bhagavad Gita

CHAPTER XIII

Arjuna:
Now would I hear, O gracious Kesava![*FN#26*]
Of Life which seems, and Soul beyond, which sees,
And what it is we know-or think to know.

Krishna:
Yea! Son of Kunti! for this flesh ye see
Is Kshetra, is the field where Life disports;
And that which views and knows it is the Soul,
Kshetrajna. In all "fields," thou Indian prince!
I am Kshetrajna. I am what surveys!
Only that knowledge knows which knows the known
By the knower![*FN#27*] What it is, that "field" of life,
What qualities it hath, and whence it is,
And why it changeth, and the faculty
That wotteth it, the mightiness of this,
And how it wotteth-hear these things from Me!
. . . .[*FN#28*]

The elements, the conscious life, the mind,
The unseen vital force, the nine strange gates
Of the body, and the five domains of sense;
Desire, dislike, pleasure and pain, and thought
Deep-woven, and persistency of being;
These all are wrought on Matter by the Soul!

Humbleness, truthfulness, and harmlessness,
Patience and honour, reverence for the wise.
Purity, constancy, control of self,
Contempt of sense-delights, self-sacrifice,
Perception of the certitude of ill
In birth, death, age, disease, suffering, and sin;
Detachment, lightly holding unto home,
Children, and wife, and all that bindeth men;

An ever-tranquil heart in fortunes good
And fortunes evil, with a will set firm
To worship Me--Me only! ceasing not;
Loving all solitudes, and shunning noise
Of foolish crowds; endeavours resolute
To reach perception of the Utmost Soul,
And grace to understand what gain it were
So to attain,--this is true Wisdom, Prince!
And what is otherwise is ignorance!

Now will I speak of knowledge best to know-
That Truth which giveth man Amrit to drink,
The Truth of HIM, the Para-Brahm, the All,
The Uncreated;; not Asat, not Sat,
Not Form, nor the Unformed; yet both, and more;--
Whose hands are everywhere, and everywhere
Planted His feet, and everywhere His eyes
Beholding, and His ears in every place
Hearing, and all His faces everywhere
Enlightening and encompassing His worlds.
Glorified in the senses He hath given,
Yet beyond sense He is; sustaining all,
Yet dwells He unattached: of forms and modes
Master, yet neither form nor mode hath He;
He is within all beings--and without--
Motionless, yet still moving; not discerned
For subtlety of instant presence; close
To all, to each; yet measurelessly far!
Not manifold, and yet subsisting still
In all which lives; for ever to be known
As the Sustainer, yet, at the End of Times,
He maketh all to end--and re-creates.
The Light of Lights He is, in the heart of the Dark
Shining eternally. Wisdom He is
And Wisdom's way, and Guide of all the wise,
Planted in every heart.

Bhagavad Gita

So have I told
Of Life's stuff, and the moulding, and the lore
To comprehend. Whoso, adoring Me,
Perceiveth this, shall surely come to Me!

Know thou that Nature and the Spirit both
Have no beginning! Know that qualities
And changes of them are by Nature wrought;
That Nature puts to work the acting frame,
But Spirit doth inform it, and so cause
Feeling of pain and pleasure. Spirit, linked
To moulded matter, entereth into bond
With qualities by Nature framed, and, thus
Married to matter, breeds the birth again
In good or evil yonis.[FN#29]

Yet is this
Yea! in its bodily prison!--Spirit pure,
Spirit supreme; surveying, governing,
Guarding, possessing; Lord and Master still
PURUSHA, Ultimate, One Soul with Me.

Whoso thus knows himself, and knows his soul
PURUSHA, working through the qualities
With Nature's modes, the light hath come for him!
Whatever flesh he bears, never again
Shall he take on its load. Some few there be
By meditation find the Soul in Self
Self-schooled; and some by long philosophy
And holy life reach thither; some by works:
Some, never so attaining, hear of light
From other lips, and seize, and cleave to it
Worshipping; yea! and those--to teaching true--
Overpass Death!

Wherever, Indian Prince!

Life is--of moving things, or things unmoved,
Plant or still seed--know, what is there hath grown
By bond of Matter and of Spirit: Know
He sees indeed who sees in all alike
The living, lordly Soul; the Soul Supreme,
Imperishable amid the Perishing:
For, whoso thus beholds, in every place,
In every form, the same, one, Living Life,
Doth no more wrongfulness unto himself,
But goes the highest road which brings to bliss.
Seeing, he sees, indeed, who sees that works
Are Nature's wont, for Soul to practise by
Acting, yet not the agent; sees the mass
Of separate living things--each of its kind--
Issue from One, and blend again to One:
Then hath he BRAHMA, he attains!

O Prince!
That Ultimate, High Spirit, Uncreate,
Unqualified, even when it entereth flesh
Taketh no stain of acts, worketh in nought!
Like to th" ethereal air, pervading all,
Which, for sheer subtlety, avoideth taint,
The subtle Soul sits everywhere, unstained:
Like to the light of the all-piercing sun
[Which is not changed by aught it shines upon,]
The Soul's light shineth pure in every place;
And they who, by such eye of wisdom, see
How Matter, and what deals with it, divide;
And how the Spirit and the flesh have strife,
Those wise ones go the way which leads to Life!

HERE ENDS CHAPTER XIII. OF THE BHAGAVAD-GITA,
Entitled "Kshetrakshetrajnavibhagayog,"
Or "The Book of Religion by Separation of Matter and Spirit."

CHAPTER XIV

Krishna:
Yet farther will I open unto thee
This wisdom of all wisdoms, uttermost,
The which possessing, all My saints have passed
To perfectness. On such high verities
Reliant, rising into fellowship
With Me, they are not born again at birth
Of Kalpas, nor at Pralyas suffer change!

This Universe the womb is where I plant
Seed of all lives! Thence, Prince of India, comes
Birth to all beings! Whoso, Kunti's Son!
Mothers each mortal form, Brahma conceives,
And I am He that fathers, sending seed!

Sattwan, Rajas, and Tamas, so are named
The qualities of Nature, "Soothfastness,"
"Passion," and "Ignorance." These three bind down
The changeless Spirit in the changeful flesh.
Whereof sweet "Soothfastness," by purity
Living unsullied and enlightened, binds
The sinless Soul to happiness and truth;
And Passion, being kin to appetite,
And breeding impulse and propensity,
Binds the embodied Soul, O Kunti's Son!
By tie of works. But Ignorance, begot
Of Darkness, blinding mortal men, binds down
Their souls to stupor, sloth, and drowsiness.
Yea, Prince of India! Soothfastness binds souls
In pleasant wise to flesh; and Passion binds
By toilsome strain; but Ignorance, which blots
The beams of wisdom, binds the soul to sloth.
Passion and Ignorance, once overcome,
Leave Soothfastness, O Bharata! Where this

With Ignorance are absent, Passion rules;
And Ignorance in hearts not good nor quick.
When at all gateways of the Body shines
The Lamp of Knowledge, then may one see well
Soothfastness settled in that city reigns;
Where longing is, and ardour, and unrest,
Impulse to strive and gain, and avarice,
Those spring from Passion--Prince!--engrained; and where
Darkness and dulness, sloth and stupor are,
'Tis Ignorance hath caused them, Kuru Chief!

Moreover, when a soul departeth, fixed
In Soothfastness, it goeth to the place--
Perfect and pure--of those that know all Truth.
If it departeth in set habitude
Of Impulse, it shall pass into the world
Of spirits tied to works; and, if it dies
In hardened Ignorance, that blinded soul
Is born anew in some unlighted womb.

The fruit of Soothfastness is true and sweet;
The fruit of lusts is pain and toil; the fruit
Of Ignorance is deeper darkness. Yea!
For Light brings light, and Passion ache to have;
And gloom, bewilderments, and ignorance
Grow forth from Ignorance. Those of the first
Rise ever higher; those of the second mode
Take a mid place; the darkened souls sink back
To lower deeps, loaded with witlessness!

When, watching life, the living man perceives
The only actors are the Qualities,
And knows what rules beyond the Qualities,
Then is he come nigh unto Me!

Bhagavad Gita

The Soul,
Thus passing forth from the Three Qualities--
Whereby arise all bodies--overcomes
Birth, Death, Sorrow, and Age; and drinketh deep
The undying wine of Amrit.

Arjuna:
Oh, my Lord!
Which be the signs to know him that hath gone
Past the Three Modes? How liveth he? What way
Leadeth him safe beyond the threefold Modes?

Krishna:
He who with equanimity surveys
Lustre of goodness, strife of passion, sloth
Of ignorance, not angry if they are,
Not wishful when they are not: he who sits
A sojourner and stranger in their midst
Unruffled, standing off, saying--serene--
When troubles break, "These be the Qualities!"
He unto whom--self-centred--grief and joy
Sound as one word; to whose deep-seeing eyes
The clod, the marble, and the gold are one;
Whose equal heart holds the same gentleness
For lovely and unlovely things, firm-set,
Well-pleased in praise and dispraise; satisfied
With honour or dishonour; unto friends
And unto foes alike in tolerance;
Detached from undertakings,--he is named
Surmounter of the Qualities!

And such--
With single, fervent faith adoring Me,
Passing beyond the Qualities, conforms
To Brahma, and attains Me!

For I am
That whereof Brahma is the likeness! Mine
The Amrit is; and Immortality
Is mine; and mine perfect Felicity!

HERE ENDS CHAPTER XIV. OF THE BHAGAVAD-GITA
Entitled "Gunatrayavibhagayog,"
Or "The Book of Religion by Separation from the Qualities."

CHAPTER XV

Krishna:
Men call the Aswattha,--the Banyan-tree,--
Which hath its boughs beneath, its roots above,--
The ever-holy tree. Yea! for its leaves
Are green and waving hymns which whisper Truth!
Who knows the Aswattha, knows Veds, and all.

Its branches shoot to heaven and sink to earth,[FN#30]
Even as the deeds of men, which take their birth
From qualities: its silver sprays and blooms,
And all the eager verdure of its girth,
Leap to quick life at kiss of sun and air,
As men's lives quicken to the temptings fair
Of wooing sense: its hanging rootlets seek
The soil beneath, helping to hold it there,

As actions wrought amid this world of men
Bind them by ever-tightening bonds again.

Bhagavad Gita

If ye knew well the teaching of the Tree,
What its shape saith; and whence it springs; and, then

How it must end, and all the ills of it,
The axe of sharp Detachment ye would whet,
And cleave the clinging snaky roots, and lay
This Aswattha of sense-life low,--to set

New growths upspringing to that happier sky,--
Which they who reach shall have no day to die,
Nor fade away, nor fall--to Him, I mean,
FATHER and FIRST, Who made the mystery

Of old Creation; for to Him come they
From passion and from dreams who break away;
Who part the bonds constraining them to flesh,
And,--Him, the Highest, worshipping alway--

No longer grow at mercy of what breeze
Of summer pleasure stirs the sleeping trees,
What blast of tempest tears them, bough and stem
To the eternal world pass such as these!

Another Sun gleams there! another Moon!
Another Light,--not Dusk, nor Dawn, nor Noon--
Which they who once behold return no more;
They have attained My rest, life's Utmost boon!

When, in this world of manifested life,
The undying Spirit, setting forth from Me,
Taketh on form, it draweth to itself
From Being's storehouse,--which containeth all,--
Senses and intellect. The Sovereign Soul
Thus entering the flesh, or quitting it,
Gathers these up, as the wind gathers scents,
Blowing above the flower-beds. Ear and Eye,

And Touch and Taste, and Smelling, these it takes,--
Yea, and a sentient mind;--linking itself
To sense-things so.

The unenlightened ones
Mark not that Spirit when he goes or comes,
Nor when he takes his pleasure in the form,
Conjoined with qualities; but those see plain
Who have the eyes to see. Holy souls see
Which strive thereto. Enlightened, they perceive
That Spirit in themselves; but foolish ones,
Even though they strive, discern not, having hearts
Unkindled, ill-informed!

Know, too, from Me
Shineth the gathered glory of the suns
Which lighten all the world: from Me the moons
Draw silvery beams, and fire fierce loveliness.
I penetrate the clay, and lend all shapes
Their living force; I glide into the plant--
Root, leaf, and bloom--to make the woodlands green
With springing sap. Becoming vital warmth,
I glow in glad, respiring frames, and pass,
With outward and with inward breath, to feed
The body by all meats.[FN#31]

For in this world
Being is twofold: the Divided, one;
The Undivided, one. All things that live
Are "the Divided." That which sits apart,
"The Undivided."

Higher still is He,
The Highest, holding all, whose Name is LORD,
The Eternal, Sovereign, First! Who fills all worlds,
Sustaining them. And--dwelling thus beyond

Divided Being and Undivided--I
Am called of men and Vedas, Life Supreme,
The PURUSHOTTAMA.

Who knows Me thus,
With mind unclouded, knoweth all, dear Prince!
And with his whole soul ever worshippeth Me.

Now is the sacred, secret Mystery
Declared to thee! Who comprehendeth this
Hath wisdom! He is quit of works in bliss!

HERE ENDS CHAPTER XV. OF THE BHAGAVAD-GITA
Entitled "Purushottamapraptiyog,"
Or "The Book of Religion by attaining the Supreme."

CHAPTER XVI

Krishna:
Fearlessness, singleness of soul, the will
Always to strive for wisdom; opened hand
And governed appetites; and piety,
And love of lonely study; humbleness,
Uprightness, heed to injure nought which lives,
Truthfulness, slowness unto wrath, a mind
That lightly letteth go what others prize;
And equanimity, and charity
Which spieth no man's faults; and tenderness

Towards all that suffer; a contented heart,
Fluttered by no desires; a bearing mild,
Modest, and grave, with manhood nobly mixed,
With patience, fortitude, and purity;
An unrevengeful spirit, never given
To rate itself too high;--such be the signs,
O Indian Prince! of him whose feet are set
On that fair path which leads to heavenly birth!

Deceitfulness, and arrogance, and pride,
Quickness to anger, harsh and evil speech,
And ignorance, to its own darkness blind,--
These be the signs, My Prince! of him whose birth
Is fated for the regions of the vile.[FN#32]

The Heavenly Birth brings to deliverance,
So should'st thou know! The birth with Asuras
Brings into bondage. Be thou joyous, Prince!
Whose lot is set apart for heavenly Birth.

Two stamps there are marked on all living men,
Divine and Undivine; I spake to thee
By what marks thou shouldst know the Heavenly Man,
Hear from me now of the Unheavenly!

They comprehend not, the Unheavenly,
How Souls go forth from Me; nor how they come
Back unto Me: nor is there Truth in these,
Nor purity, nor rule of Life. "This world
Hath not a Law, nor Order, nor a Lord,"
So say they: "nor hath risen up by Cause
Following on Cause, in perfect purposing,
But is none other than a House of Lust."
And, this thing thinking, all those ruined ones--
Of little wit, dark-minded--give themselves
To evil deeds, the curses of their kind.

Bhagavad Gita

Surrendered to desires insatiable,
Full of deceitfulness, folly, and pride,
In blindness cleaving to their errors, caught
Into the sinful course, they trust this lie
As it were true--this lie which leads to death--
Finding in Pleasure all the good which is,
And crying "Here it finisheth!"

Ensnared
In nooses of a hundred idle hopes,
Slaves to their passion and their wrath, they buy
Wealth with base deeds, to glut hot appetites;
"Thus much, to-day," they say, "we gained! thereby
Such and such wish of heart shall have its fill;
And this is ours! and th' other shall be ours!
To-day we slew a foe, and we will slay
Our other enemy to-morrow! Look!
Are we not lords? Make we not goodly cheer?
Is not our fortune famous, brave, and great?
Rich are we, proudly born! What other men
Live like to us? Kill, then, for sacrifice!
Cast largesse, and be merry!" So they speak
Darkened by ignorance; and so they fall--
Tossed to and fro with projects, tricked, and bound
In net of black delusion, lost in lusts--
Down to foul Naraka. Conceited, fond,
Stubborn and proud, dead-drunken with the wine
Of wealth, and reckless, all their offerings
Have but a show of reverence, being not made
In piety of ancient faith. Thus vowed
To self-hood, force, insolence, feasting, wrath,
These My blasphemers, in the forms they wear
And in the forms they breed, my foemen are,
Hateful and hating; cruel, evil, vile,
Lowest and least of men, whom I cast down
Again, and yet again, at end of lives,

Into some devilish womb, whence--birth by birth--
The devilish wombs re-spawn them, all beguiled;
And, till they find and worship Me, sweet Prince!
Tread they that Nether Road.

The Doors of Hell
Are threefold, whereby men to ruin pass,--
The door of Lust, the door of Wrath, the door
Of Avarice. Let a man shun those three!
He who shall turn aside from entering
All those three gates of Narak, wendeth straight
To find his peace, and comes to Swarga's gate.

. . . .*[FN#33]*

HERE ENDETH CHAPTER XVI. OF THE BHAGAVAD-GITA,
Entitled "Daivasarasaupadwibhagayog,"
Or "The Book of the Separateness of the Divine and Undivine."

CHAPTER XVII

Arjuna:
If men forsake the holy ordinance,
Heedless of Shastras, yet keep faith at heart
And worship, what shall be the state of those,
Great Krishna! Sattwan, Rajas, Tamas? Say!

Bhagavad Gita

Krishna:
Threefold the faith is of mankind and springs
From those three qualities,--becoming "true,"
Or "passion-stained," or "dark," as thou shalt hear!

The faith of each believer, Indian Prince!
Conforms itself to what he truly is.
Where thou shalt see a worshipper, that one
To what he worships lives assimilate,
[Such as the shrine, so is the votary,]
The "soothfast" souls adore true gods; the souls
Obeying Rajas worship Rakshasas[FN#34]
Or Yakshas; and the men of Darkness pray
To Pretas and to Bhutas.[FN#35] Yea, and those
Who practise bitter penance, not enjoined
By rightful rule--penance which hath its root
In self-sufficient, proud hypocrisies--
Those men, passion-beset, violent, wild,
Torturing--the witless ones--My elements
Shut in fair company within their flesh,
(Nay, Me myself, present within the flesh!)
Know them to devils devoted, not to Heaven!
For like as foods are threefold for mankind
In nourishing, so is there threefold way
Of worship, abstinence, and almsgiving!
Hear this of Me! there is a food which brings
Force, substance, strength, and health, and joy to live,
Being well-seasoned, cordial, comforting,
The "Soothfast" meat. And there be foods which bring
Aches and unrests, and burning blood, and grief,
Being too biting, heating, salt, and sharp,
And therefore craved by too strong appetite.
And there is foul food--kept from over-night,[FN#36]
Savourless, filthy, which the foul will eat,
A feast of rottenness, meet for the lips
Of such as love the "Darkness."

Thus with rites;--
A sacrifice not for rewardment made,
Offered in rightful wise, when he who vows
Sayeth, with heart devout, "This I should do!"
Is "Soothfast" rite. But sacrifice for gain,
Offered for good repute, be sure that this,
O Best of Bharatas! is Rajas-rite,
With stamp of "passion." And a sacrifice
Offered against the laws, with no due dole
Of food-giving, with no accompaniment
Of hallowed hymn, nor largesse to the priests,
In faithless celebration, call it vile,
The deed of "Darkness!"--lost!

Worship of gods
Meriting worship; lowly reverence
Of Twice-borns, Teachers, Elders; Purity,
Rectitude, and the Brahmacharya's vow,
And not to injure any helpless thing,--
These make a true religiousness of Act.

Words causing no man woe, words ever true,
Gentle and pleasing words, and those ye say
In murmured reading of a Sacred Writ,--
These make the true religiousness of Speech.

Serenity of soul, benignity,
Sway of the silent Spirit, constant stress
To sanctify the Nature,--these things make
Good rite, and true religiousness of Mind.

Such threefold faith, in highest piety
Kept, with no hope of gain, by hearts devote,
Is perfect work of Sattwan, true belief.

Religion shown in act of proud display

Bhagavad Gita

To win good entertainment, worship, fame,
Such--say I--is of Rajas, rash and vain.

Religion followed by a witless will
To torture self, or come at power to hurt
Another,--'tis of Tamas, dark and ill.

The gift lovingly given, when one shall say
"Now must I gladly give!" when he who takes
Can render nothing back; made in due place,
Due time, and to a meet recipient,
Is gift of Sattwan, fair and profitable.

The gift selfishly given, where to receive
Is hoped again, or when some end is sought,
Or where the gift is proffered with a grudge,
This is of Rajas, stained with impulse, ill.

The gift churlishly flung, at evil time,
In wrongful place, to base recipient,
Made in disdain or harsh unkindliness,
Is gift of Tamas, dark; it doth not bless![*FN#37*]

HERE ENDETH CHAPTER XVII. OF THE BHAGAVAD-GITA,
Entitled "Sraddhatrayavibhagayog,"
Or "The Book of Religion by the Threefold Kinds of Faith."

CHAPTER XVIII

Arjuna:
Fain would I better know, Thou Glorious One!
The very truth--Heart's Lord!--of Sannyas,
 Abstention; and enunciation, Lord!
 Tyaga; and what separates these twain!

Krishna:
The poets rightly teach that Sannyas
Is the foregoing of all acts which spring
 Out of desire; and their wisest say
 Tyaga is renouncing fruit of acts.

There be among the saints some who have held
 All action sinful, and to be renounced;
And some who answer, "Nay! the goodly acts--
As worship, penance, alms--must be performed!"
 Hear now My sentence, Best of Bharatas!

'Tis well set forth, O Chaser of thy Foes!
 Renunciation is of threefold form,
And Worship, Penance, Alms, not to be stayed;
 Nay, to be gladly done; for all those three
 Are purifying waters for true souls!

Yet must be practised even those high works
 In yielding up attachment, and all fruit
Produced by works. This is My judgment, Prince!
 This My insuperable and fixed decree!

Abstaining from a work by right prescribed
 Never is meet! So to abstain doth spring
 From "Darkness," and Delusion teacheth it.
 Abstaining from a work grievous to flesh,
When one saith "'Tisunpleasing!" this is null!

Bhagavad Gita

Such an one acts from "passion;" nought of gain
Wins his Renunciation! But, Arjun!
Abstaining from attachment to the work,
Abstaining from rewardment in the work,
While yet one doeth it full faithfully,
Saying, "Tis right to do!" that is "true " act
And abstinence! Who doeth duties so,
Unvexed if his work fail, if it succeed
Unflattered, in his own heart justified,
Quit of debates and doubts, his is "true" act:
For, being in the body, none may stand
Wholly aloof from act; yet, who abstains
From profit of his acts is abstinent.

The fruit of labours, in the lives to come,
Is threefold for all men,--Desirable,
And Undesirable, and mixed of both;
But no fruit is at all where no work was.

Hear from me, Long-armed Lord! the makings five
Which go to every act, in Sankhya taught
As necessary. First the force; and then
The agent; next, the various instruments;
Fourth, the especial effort; fifth, the God.
What work soever any mortal doth
Of body, mind, or speech, evil or good,
By these five doth he that. Which being thus,
Whoso, for lack of knowledge, seeth himself
As the sole actor, knoweth nought at all
And seeth nought. Therefore, I say, if one--
Holding aloof from self--with unstained mind
Should slay all yonder host, being bid to slay,
He doth not slay; he is not bound thereby!

Knowledge, the thing known, and the mind which knows,
These make the threefold starting-ground of act.

The act, the actor, and the instrument,
These make the threefold total of the deed.
But knowledge, agent, act, are differenced
By three dividing qualities. Hear now
Which be the qualities dividing them.

There is "true" Knowledge. Learn thou it is this:
To see one changeless Life in all the Lives,
And in the Separate, One Inseparable.
There is imperfect Knowledge: that which sees
The separate existences apart,
And, being separated, holds them real.
There is false Knowledge: that which blindly clings
To one as if 'twere all, seeking no Cause,
Deprived of light, narrow, and dull, and "dark."
There is "right" Action: that which being enjoined--
Is wrought without attachment, passionlessly,
For duty, not for love, nor hate, nor gain.
There is "vain" Action: that which men pursue
Aching to satisfy desires, impelled
By sense of self, with all-absorbing stress:
This is of Rajas--passionate and vain.
There is "dark" Action: when one doth a thing
Heedless of issues, heedless of the hurt
Or wrong for others, heedless if he harm
His own soul--'tis of Tamas, black and bad!

There is the "rightful"doer. He who acts
Free from self-seeking, humble, resolute,
Steadfast, in good or evil hap the same,
Content to do aright-he "truly" acts.
There is th' "impassioned" doer. He that works
From impulse, seeking profit, rude and bold
To overcome, unchastened; slave by turns
Of sorrow and of joy: of Rajas he!
And there be evil doers; loose of heart,

Bhagavad Gita

Low-minded, stubborn, fraudulent, remiss,
Dull, slow, despondent--children of the "dark."

Hear, too, of Intellect and Steadfastness
The threefold separation, Conqueror-Prince!
How these are set apart by Qualities.

Good is the Intellect which comprehends
The coming forth and going back of life,
What must be done, and what must not be done,
What should be feared, and what should not be feared,
What binds and what emancipates the soul:
That is of Sattwan, Prince! of "soothfastness."
Marred is the Intellect which, knowing right
And knowing wrong, and what is well to do
And what must not be done, yet understands
Nought with firm mind, nor as the calm truth is:
This is of Rajas, Prince! and "passionate!"
Evil is Intellect which, wrapped in gloom,
Looks upon wrong as right, and sees all things
Contrariwise of Truth. O Pritha's Son!
That is of Tamas, "dark" and desperate!

Good is the steadfastness whereby a man
Masters his beats of heart, his very breath
Of life, the action of his senses; fixed
In never-shaken faith and piety:
That is of Sattwan, Prince! "soothfast" and fair!
Stained is the steadfastness whereby a man
Holds to his duty, purpose, effort, end,
For life's sake, and the love of goods to gain,
Arjuna! 'tis of Rajas, passion-stamped!
Sad is the steadfastness wherewith the fool
Cleaves to his sloth, his sorrow, and his fears,
His folly and despair. This--Pritha's Son!--
Is born of Tamas, "dark" and miserable!

Hear further, Chief of Bharatas! from Me
The threefold kinds of Pleasure which there be.

Good Pleasure is the pleasure that endures,
Banishing pain for aye; bitter at first
As poison to the soul, but afterward
Sweet as the taste of Amrit. Drink of that!
It springeth in the Spirit's deep content.
And painful Pleasure springeth from the bond
Between the senses and the sense-world. Sweet
As Amrit is its first taste, but its last
Bitter as poison. 'Tis of Rajas, Prince!
And foul and "dark" the Pleasure is which springs
From sloth and sin and foolishness; at first
And at the last, and all the way of life
The soul bewildering. 'Tis of Tamas, Prince!

For nothing lives on earth, nor 'midst the gods
In utmost heaven, but hath its being bound
With these three Qualities, by Nature framed.

The work of Brahmans, Kshatriyas, Vaisyas,
And Sudras, O thou Slayer of thy Foes!
Is fixed by reason of the Qualities
Planted in each:

A Brahman's virtues, Prince!
Born of his nature, are serenity,
Self-mastery, religion, purity,
Patience, uprightness, learning, and to know
The truth of things which be. A Kshatriya's pride,
Born of his nature, lives in valour, fire,
Constancy, skilfulness, spirit in fight,
And open-handedness and noble mien,
As of a lord of men. A Vaisya's task,
Born with his nature, is to till the ground,

Bhagavad Gita

Tend cattle, venture trade. A Sudra's state,
Suiting his nature, is to minister.

Whoso performeth--diligent, content--
The work allotted him, whate'er it be,
Lays hold of perfectness! Hear how a man
Findeth perfection, being so content:
He findeth it through worship--wrought by work--
Of Him that is the Source of all which lives,
Of HIM by Whom the universe was stretched.

Better thine own work is, though done with fault,
Than doing others' work, ev'n excellently.
He shall not fall in sin who fronts the task
Set him by Nature's hand! Let no man leave
His natural duty, Prince! though it bear blame!
For every work hath blame, as every flame
Is wrapped in smoke! Only that man attains
Perfect surcease of work whose work was wrought
With mind unfettered, soul wholly subdued,
Desires for ever dead, results renounced.

Learn from me, Son of Kunti! also this,
How one, attaining perfect peace, attains
BRAHM, the supreme, the highest height of all!

Devoted--with a heart grown pure, restrained
In lordly self-control, forgoing wiles
Of song and senses, freed from love and hate,
Dwelling 'mid solitudes, in diet spare,
With body, speech, and will tamed to obey,
Ever to holy meditation vowed,
From passions liberate, quit of the Self,
Of arrogance, impatience, anger, pride;
Freed from surroundings, quiet, lacking nought--
Such an one grows to oneness with the BRAHM;

Such an one, growing one with BRAHM, serene,
Sorrows no more, desires no more; his soul,
Equally loving all that lives, loves well
Me, Who have made them, and attains to Me.
By this same love and worship doth he know
Me as I am, how high and wonderful,
And knowing, straightway enters into Me.
And whatsoever deeds he doeth--fixed
In Me, as in his refuge--he hath won
For ever and for ever by My grace
Th' Eternal Rest! So win thou! In thy thoughts
Do all thou dost for Me! Renounce for Me!
Sacrifice heart and mind and will to Me!
Live in the faith of Me! In faith of Me
All dangers thou shalt vanquish, by My grace;
But, trusting to thyself and heeding not,
Thou can'st but perish! If this day thou say'st,
Relying on thyself, "I will not fight!"
Vain will the purpose prove! thy qualities
Would spur thee to the war. What thou dost shun,
Misled by fair illusions, thou wouldst seek
Against thy will, when the task comes to thee
Waking the promptings in thy nature set.
There lives a Master in the hearts of men
Maketh their deeds, by subtle pulling--strings,
Dance to what tune HE will. With all thy soul
Trust Him, and take Him for thy succour, Prince!
So--only so, Arjuna!--shalt thou gain--
By grace of Him--the uttermost repose,
The Eternal Place!

Thus hath been opened thee
This Truth of Truths, the Mystery more hid
Than any secret mystery. Meditate!
And--as thou wilt--then act!

Bhagavad Gita

Nay! but once more
Take My last word, My utmost meaning have!
Precious thou art to Me; right well-beloved!
Listen! I tell thee for thy comfort this.
Give Me thy heart! adore Me! serve Me! cling
In faith and love and reverence to Me!
So shalt thou come to Me! I promise true,
For thou art sweet to Me!

And let go those--
Rites and writ duties! Fly to Me alone!
Make Me thy single refuge! I will free
Thy soul from all its sins! Be of good cheer!
[Hide, the holy Krishna saith,
This from him that hath no faith,
Him that worships not, nor seeks
Wisdom's teaching when she speaks:
Hide it from all men who mock;
But, wherever, 'mid the flock
Of My lovers, one shall teach
This divinest, wisest, speech--
Teaching in the faith to bring
Truth to them, and offering
Of all honour unto Me--
Unto Brahma cometh he!
Nay, and nowhere shall ye find
Any man of all mankind
Doing dearer deed for Me;
Nor shall any dearer be
In My earth. Yea, furthermore,
Whoso reads this converse o'er,
Held by Us upon the plain,
Pondering piously and fain,
He hath paid Me sacrifice!
(Krishna speaketh in this wise!)
Yea, and whoso, full of faith,

Heareth wisely what it saith,
Heareth meekly,--when he dies,
Surely shall his spirit rise
To those regions where the Blest,
Free of flesh, in joyance rest.]

Hath this been heard by thee, O Indian Prince!
With mind intent? hath all the ignorance--
Which bred thy trouble--vanished, My Arjun?

Arjuna:
Trouble and ignorance are gone! the Light
Hath come unto me, by Thy favour, Lord!
Now am I fixed! my doubt is fled away!
According to Thy word, so will I do!

Sanjaya:
Thus gathered I the gracious speech of Krishna, O my King!
Thus have I told, with heart a-thrill, this wise and wondrous thing
By great Vyasa's learning writ, how Krishna's self made known
The Yoga, being Yoga's Lord. So is the high truth shown!
And aye, when I remember, O Lord my King, again
Arjuna and the God in talk, and all this holy strain,
Great is my gladness: when I muse that splendour, passing speech,
Of Hari, visible and plain, there is no tongue to reach
My marvel and my love and bliss. O Archer-Prince! all hail!
O Krishna, Lord of Yoga! surely there shall not fail
Blessing, and victory, and power, for Thy most mighty sake,
Where this song comes of Arjun, and how with God he spake.

HERE ENDS, WITH CHAPTER XVIII.,
Entitled "Mokshasanyasayog,"
Or "The Book of Religion by Deliverance and Renunciation,"

THE BHAGAVAD-GITA.

[FN#1] Some repetitionary lines are here omitted.
[FN#2] Technical phrases of Vedic religion.
[FN#3] The whole of this passage is highly involved and difficult to render.
[FN#4] I feel convinced sankhyanan and yoginan must be transposed here in sense.
[FN#5] I am doubtful of accuracy here.
[FN#6] A name of the sun.
[FN#7] Without desire of fruit.
[FN#8] That is,"joy and sorrow, success and failure, heat and cold,"&c.
[FN#9] i.e., the body.
[FN#10] The Sanskrit has this play on the double meaning of Atman.
[FN#11] So in original.
[FN#12] Beings of low and devilish nature.
[FN#13] Krishna.
[FN#14] I read here janma, "birth;" not jara,"age"
[FN#15] I have discarded ten lines of Sanskrit text here as an undoubted interpolation by some Vedantist
[FN#16] The Sanskrit poem here rises to an elevation of style and manner which I have endeavoured to mark by change of metre.
[FN#17] Ahinsa.
[FN#18] The nectar of immortality.
[FN#19] Called "The Jap."
[FN#20] The compound form of Sanskrit words.
[FN#21] "Kamalapatraksha"
[FN#22] These are all divine or deified orders of the Hindoo Pantheon.
[FN#23] "Hail to Thee, God of Gods! Be favourable!"
[FN#24] The wind.
[FN#25] "Not peering about,"anapeksha.
[FN#26] The Calcutta edition of the Mahabharata has these three

opening lines.

[FN#27] This is the nearest possible version of Kshetrakshetrajnayojnanan yat tajnan matan mama.

[FN#28] I omit two lines of the Sanskrit here, evidently interpolated by some Vedantist.

[FN#29] Wombs.

[FN#30] I do not consider the Sanskrit verses here-which are somewhat
freely rendered--"an attack on the authority of the Vedas," with Mr Davies, but a beautiful lyrical episode, a new "Parable of the fig-tree."

[FN#31] I omit a verse here, evidently interpolated.

[FN#32] "Of the Asuras,"lit.

[FN#33] I omit the ten concluding shlokas, with Mr Davis.

[FN#34] Rakshasas and Yakshas are unembodied but capricious beings of great power, gifts, and beauty, same times also of benignity.

[FN#35] These are spirits of evil wandering ghosts.

[FN#36] Yatayaman, food which has remained after the watches of the night. In India this would probably "go bad."

[FN#37] I omit the concluding shlokas, as of very doubtful authenticity.

Bhagavad Gita

THE LIGHT OF ASIA

By Sir Edwin Arnold

This volume is dutifully inscribed to the Sovereign, Grand Master, and Companions of The Most Exalted Order of the Star of India by The Author.

The Light Of Asia

Book The First

 The Scripture of the Saviour of the World,
Lord Buddha--Prince Siddartha styled on earth
In Earth and Heavens and Hells Incomparable,
 All-honoured, Wisest, Best, most Pitiful;
 The Teacher of Nirvana and the Law.

 Then came he to be born again for men.

 Below the highest sphere four Regents sit
Who rule our world, and under them are zones
Nearer, but high, where saintliest spirits dead
Wait thrice ten thousand years, then live again;
 And on Lord Buddha, waiting in that sky,
Came for our sakes the five sure signs of birth
 So that the Devas knew the signs, and said
 "Buddha will go again to help the World."
"Yea!" spake He, "now I go to help the World.
This last of many times; for birth and death
End hence for me and those who learn my Law.
 I will go down among the Sakyas,
 Under the southward snows of Himalay,
Where pious people live and a just King."

 That night the wife of King Suddhodana,
 Maya the Queen, asleep beside her Lord,
Dreamed a strange dream; dreamed that a star
    from heaven--
Splendid, six-rayed, in colour rosy-pearl,
 Whereof the token was an Elephant
 Six-tusked and whiter than Vahuka's milk--
Shot through the void and, shining into her,
Entered her womb upon the right. Awaked,
Bliss beyond mortal mother's filled her breast,

And over half the earth a lovely light
Forewent the morn. The strong hills shook; the waves
Sank lulled; all flowers that blow by day came forth
As 't were high noon; down to the farthest hells
Passed the Queen's joy, as when warm sunshine thrills
Wood-glooms to gold, and into all the deeps
A tender whisper pierced. "Oh ye," it said,
"The dead that are to live, the live who die,
Uprise, and hear, and hope! Buddha is come!"
Whereat in Limbos numberless much peace
Spread, and the world's heart throbbed, and a wind blew
With unknown freshness over lands and seas.
And when the morning dawned, and this was told,
The grey dream-readers said "The dream is good!
The Crab is in conjunction with the Sun;
The Queen shall bear a boy, a holy child
Of wondrous wisdom, profiting all flesh,
Who shall deliver men from ignorance,
Or rule the world, if he will deign to rule."

In this wise was the holy Buddha born.

Queen Maya stood at noon, her days fulfilled,
Under a Palsa in the Palace-grounds,
A stately trunk, straight as a temple-shaft,
With crown of glossy leaves and fragrant blooms;
And, knowing the time some--for all things knew--
The conscious tree bent down its boughs to make
A bower above Queen Maya's majesty,
And Earth put forth a thousand sudden flowers
To spread a couch, while, ready for the bath,
The rock hard by gave out a limpid stream
Of crystal flow. So brought she forth her child
Pangless--he having on his perfect form
The marks, thirty and two, of blessed birth;
Of which the great news to the Palace came.

The Light Of Asia

But when they brought the painted palanquin
To fetch him home, the bearers of the poles
Were the four Regents of the Earth, come down
From Mount Sumeru--they who write men's deeds
On brazen plates--the Angel of the East,
Whose hosts are clad in silver robes, and bear
Targets of pearl: the Angel of the South,
Whose horsemen, the Kumbhandas, ride blue steeds,
With sapphire shields: the Angel of the West,
By Nagas followed, riding steeds blood-red,
With coral shields: the Angel of the North,
Environed by his Yakshas, all in gold,
On yellow horses, bearing shields of gold.
These, with their pomp invisible, came down
And took the poles, in caste and outward garb
Like bearers, yet most mighty gods; and gods
Walked free with men that day, though men knew not
For Heaven was filled with gladness for Earth's sake,
Knowing Lord Buddha thus was come again.

But King Suddhodana wist not of this;
The portents troubled, till his dream-readers
Augured a Prince of earthly dominance,
A Chakravartin, such as rise to rule
Once in each thousand years; seven gifts he has
The Chakra-ratna, disc divine; the gem;
The horse, the Aswa-ratna, that proud steed
Which tramps the clouds; a snow-white elephant,
The Hasti-ratna, born to bear his King;
The crafty Minister, the General
Unconquered, and the wife of peerless grace,
The Istri-ratna, lovelier than the Dawn.
For which gifts looking with this wondrous boy,
The King gave order that his town should keep
High festival; therefore the ways were swept,
Rose-odours sprinkled in the street, the trees

Were hung with lamps and flags, while merry crowds
    Gaped on the sword-players and posturers,
The jugglers, charmers, swingers, rope-walkers,
The nautch-girls in their spangled skirts and bells
That chime light laughter round their restless feet;
    The masquers wrapped in skins of bear and deer.
      The tiger-tamers, wrestlers, quail-fighters,
      Beaters of drum and twanglers of the wire,
      Who made the people happy by command.
    Moreover from afar came merchant-men,
    Bringing, on tidings of this birth, rich gifts
In golden trays; goat-shawls, and nard and jade,
Turkises, "evening-sky" tint, woven webs--
So fine twelve folds hide not a modest face--
Waist-cloths sewn thick with pearls, and sandalwood;
    Homage from tribute cities; so they called
    Their Prince Svarthasiddh, "All-Prospering,"
        Briefer, Siddartha.

        'Mongst the strangers came
A grey-haired saint, Asita, one whose ears,
Long closed to earthly things, caught heavenly sounds,
    And heard at prayer beneath his peepul-tree
    The Devas singing songs at Buddha's birth.
    Wondrous in lore he was by age and fasts;
    Him, drawing nigh, seeming so reverend,
    The King saluted, and Queen Maya made
    To lay her babe before such holy feet;
But when he saw the Prince the old man cried
    "Ah, Queen, not so!" and thereupon he touched
Eight times the dust, laid his waste visage there,
    Saying, "O Babe! I worship! Thou art He!
    I see the rosy light, the foot-sole marks,
    The soft curled tendril of the Swastika,
    The sacred primal signs thirty and two,
    The eighty lesser tokens. Thou art Buddh,

The Light Of Asia

And thou wilt preach the Law and save all flesh
Who learn the Law, though I shall never hear,
Dying too soon, who lately longed to die;
Howbeit I have seen Thee. Know, O King!
This is that Blossom on our human tree
Which opens once in many myriad years--
But opened, fills the world with Wisdom's scent
And Love's dropped honey; from thy royal root
A Heavenly Lotus springs: Ah, happy House!
Yet not all-happy, for a sword must pierce
Thy bowels for this boy--whilst thou, sweet Queen!
Dear to all gods and men for this great birth,
Henceforth art grown too sacred for more woe,
And life is woe, therefore in seven days
Painless thou shalt attain the close of pain."

Which fell: for on the seventh evening
Queen Maya smiling slept, and waked no more,
Passing content to Trayastrinshas-Heaven,
Where countless Devas worship her and wait
Attendant on that radiant Motherhead.
But for the Babe they found a foster-nurse,
Princess Mahaprajapati--her breast
Nourished with noble milk the lips of
Him Whose lips comfort the Worlds.

When th' eighth year passed
The careful King bethought to teach his son
All that a Prince should learn, for still he shunned
The too vast presage of those miracles,
The glories and the sufferings of a Buddh.
So, in full council of his Ministers,
"Who is the wisest man, great sirs," he asked,
"To teach my Prince that which a Prince should know?"
Whereto gave answer each with instant voice
"King! Viswamitra is the wisest one,

The farthest-seen in Scriptures, and the best
In learning, and the manual arts, and all."
Thus Viswamitra came and heard commands;
And, on a day found fortunate, the Prince
Took up his slate of ox-red sandal-wood,
All-beautified by gems around the rim,
And sprinkled smooth with dust of emery,
These took he, and his writing-stick, and stood
With eyes bent down before the Sage, who said,
"Child, write this Scripture, speaking slow the verse
'Gayatri' named, which only High-born hear:--

"Om, tatsaviturvarenyam
Bhargo devasya dhimahi
Dhiyo yo na prachodayat."

"Acharya, I write," meekly replied
The Prince, and quickly on the dust he drew--
Not in one script, but many characters
The sacred verse; Nagri and Dakshin, Ni,
Mangal, Parusha, Yava, Tirthi, Uk,
Darad, Sikhyani, Mana, Madhyachar,
The pictured writings and the speech of signs,
Tokens of cave-men and the sea-peoples,
Of those who worship snakes beneath the earth,
And those who flame adore and the sun's orb,
The Magians and the dwellers on the mounds;
Of all the nations all strange scripts he traced
One after other with his writing-stick.
Reading the master's verse in every tongue;
And Viswamitra said, "It is enough,
Let us to numbers.

"After me repeat
Your numeration till we reach the Lakh,
One, two, three, four, to ten, and then by tens

The Light Of Asia

To hundreds, thousands." After him the child
Named digits, decads, centuries; nor paused,
The round Lakh reached, but softly murmured on
"Then comes the koti, nahut, ninnahut,
Khamba, viskhamba, abab, attata,
To kumuds, gundhikas, and utpalas,
By pundarikas unto padumas,
Which last is how you count the utmost grains
Of Hastagiri ground to finest dust;
But beyond that a numeration is,
The Katha, used to count the stars of night;
The Koti-Katha, for the ocean drops;
Ingga, the calculus of circulars;
Sarvanikchepa, by the which you deal
With all the sands of Gunga, till we come
To Antah-Kalpas, where the unit is
The sands of ten crore Gungas. If one seeks
More comprehensive scale, th' arithmic mounts
By the Asankya, which is the tale
Of all the drops that in ten thousand years
Would fall on all the worlds by daily rain;
Thence unto Maha Kalpas, by the which
The Gods compute their future and their past."

"'Tis good," the Sage rejoined, "Most noble Prince,
If these thou know'st, needs it that I should teach
The mensuration of the lineal?"
Humbly the boy replied, "Acharya!"
"Be pleased to hear me. Paramanus ten
A parasukshma make; ten of those build
The trasarene, and seven trasarenes
One mote's-length floating in the beam, seven motes
The whisker-point of mouse, and ten of these
One likhya; likhyas ten a yuka, ten
Yukas a heart of barley, which is held
Seven times a wasp-waist; so unto the grain

Of mung and mustard and the barley-corn,
Whereof ten give the finger joint, twelve joints
The span, wherefrom we reach the cubit, staff,
Bow-length, lance-length; while twenty lengths of lance
Mete what is named a 'breath,' which is to say
Such space as man may stride with lungs once filled,
Whereof a gow is forty, four times that
A yojana; and, Master! if it please,
I shall recite how many sun-motes lie
From end to end within a yojana."
Thereat, with instant skill, the little Prince
Pronounced the total of the atoms true.
But Viswamitra heard it on his face
Prostrate before the boy; "For thou," he cried,
"Art Teacher of thy teachers--thou, not I,
Art Guru. Oh, I worship thee, sweet Prince!
That comest to my school only to show
Thou knowest all without the books, and know'st
Fair reverence besides."

Which reverence
Lord Buddha kept to all his schoolmasters,
Albeit beyond their learning taught; in speech
Right gentle, yet so wise; princely of mien,
Yet softly-mannered; modest, deferent,
And tender-hearted, though of fearless blood;
No bolder horseman in the youthful band
E'er rode in gay chase of the shy gazelles;
No keener driver of the chariot
In mimic contest scoured the Palace-courts;
Yet in mid-play the boy would ofttimes pause,
Letting the deer pass free; would ofttimes yield
His half-won race because the labouring steeds
Fetched painful breath; or if his princely mates
Saddened to lose, or if some wistful dream
Swept o'er his thoughts. And ever with the years

The Light Of Asia

Waxed this compassionateness of our Lord,
Even as a great tree grows from two soft leaves
To spread its shade afar; but hardly yet
Knew the young child of sorrow, pain, or tears,
Save as strange names for things not felt by kings,
Nor ever to be felt. But it befell
In the Royal garden on a day of spring,
A flock of wild swans passed, voyaging north
To their nest-places on Himala's breast.
Calling in love-notes down their snowy line
The bright birds flew, by fond love piloted;
And Devadatta, cousin of the Prince,
Pointed his bow, and loosed a wilful shaft
Which found the wide wing of the foremost swan
Broad-spread to glide upon the free blue road,
So that it fell, the bitter arrow fixed,
Bright scarlet blood-gouts staining the pure plumes.
Which seeing, Prince Siddartha took the bird
Tenderly up, rested it in his lap
Sitting with knees crossed, as Lord Buddha sits
And, soothing with a touch the wild thing's fright,
Composed its ruffled vans, calmed its quick heart,
Caressed it into peace with light kind palms
As soft as plantain-leaves an hour unrolled;
And while the left hand held, the right hand drew
The cruel steel forth from the wound and laid
Cool leaves and healing honey on the smart.
Yet all so little knew the boy of pain
That curiously into his wrist he pressed
The arrow's barb, and winced to feel it sting,
And turned with tears to soothe his bird again.

Then some one came who said, "My Prince hath shot
A swan, which fell among the roses here,
He bids me pray you send it. Will you send?"
"Nay," quoth Siddartha, "if the bird were dead

To send it to the slayer might be well,
But the swan lives; my cousin hath but killed
The god-like speed which throbbed in this white wing."
And Devadatta answered, "The wild thing,
Living or dead, is his who fetched it down;
'T was no man's in the clouds, but fall'n 't is mine,
Give me my prize, fair Cousin." Then our Lord
Laid the swan's neck beside his own smooth cheek
And gravely spake, "Say no! the bird is mine,
The first of myriad things which shall be mine
By right of mercy and love's lordliness.
For now I know, by what within me stirs,
That I shall teach compassion unto men
And be a speechless world's interpreter,
Abating this accursed flood of woe,
Not man's alone; but, if the Prince disputes,
Let him submit this matter to the wise
And we will wait their word." So was it done;
In full divan the business had debate,
And many thought this thing and many that,
Till there arose an unknown priest who said,
"If life be aught, the saviour of a life
Owns more the living thing than be can own
Who sought to slay--the slayer spoils and wastes,
The cherisher sustains, give him the bird:"
Which judgment all found just; but when the King
Sought out the sage for honour, he was gone;
And some one saw a hooded snake glide forth,--
The gods come ofttimes thus! So our Lord Buddh
Began his works of mercy.

Yet not more
Knew he as yet of grief than that one bird's,
Which, being healed, went joyous to its kind.
But on another day the King said, "Come,
Sweet son! and see the pleasaunce of the spring,

The Light Of Asia

And how the fruitful earth is wooed to yield
Its riches to the reaper; how my realm--
Which shall be thine when the pile flames for me--
Feeds all its mouths and keeps the King's chest filled.
Fair is the season with new leaves, bright blooms,
Green grass, and cries of plough-time." So they rode
Into a lane of wells and gardens, where,
All up and down the rich red loam, the steers
Strained their strong shoulders in the creaking yoke
Dragging the ploughs; the fat soil rose and rolled
In smooth dark waves back from the plough; who drove
Planted both feet upon the leaping share
To make the furrow deep; among the palms
The tinkle of the rippling water rang,
And where it ran the glad earth 'broidered it
With balsams and the spears of lemon-grass.
Elsewhere were sowers who went forth to sow;
And all the jungle laughed with nesting-songs,
And all the thickets rustled with small life
Of lizard, bee, beetle, and creeping things
Pleased at the spring-time. In the mango-sprays
The sun-birds flashed; alone at his green forge
Toiled the loud coppersmith; bee-eaters hawked
Chasing the purple butterflies; beneath,
Striped squirrels raced, the mynas perked and picked,
The nine brown sisters chattered in the thorn,
The pied fish-tiger hung above the pool,
The egrets stalked among the buffaloes,
The kites sailed circles in the golden air;
About the painted temple peacocks flew,
The blue doves cooed from every well, far off
The village drums beat for some marriage-feast;
All things spoke peace and plenty, and the Prince
Saw and rejoiced. But, looking deep, he saw
The thorns which grow upon this rose of life
How the sweat peasant sweated for his wage,

Toiling for leave to live; and how he urged
The great-eyed oxen through the flaming hours,
Goading their velvet flanks: then marked he, too,
How lizard fed on ant, and snake on him,
And kite on both; and how the fish-hawk robbed
The fish-tiger of that which it had seized;
The shrike chasing the bulbul, which did chase
The jewelled butterflies; till everywhere
Each slew a slayer and in turn was slain,
Life living upon death. So the fair show
Veiled one vast, savage, grim conspiracy
Of mutual murder, from the worm to man,
Who himself kills his fellow; seeing which--
The hungry ploughman and his labouring kine,
Their dewlaps blistered with the bitter yoke,
The rage to live which makes all living strife--
The Prince Siddartha sighed. "In this," he said,
"That happy earth they brought me forth to see?
How salt with sweat the peasant's bread! how hard
The oxen's service! in the brake how fierce
The war of weak and strong! i' th' air what plots!
No refuge e'en in water. Go aside
A space, and let me muse on what ye show."
So saying, the good Lord Buddha seated him
Under a jambu-tree, with ankles crossed--
As holy statues sit--and first began
To meditate this deep disease of life,
What its far source and whence its remedy.
So vast a pity filled him, such wide love
For living things, such passion to heal pain,
That by their stress his princely spirit passed
To ecstasy, and, purged from mortal taint
Of sense and self, the boy attained thereat
Dhyana, first step of "the path."

There flew
High overhead that hour five holy ones,
Whose free wings faltered as they passed the tree.
"What power superior draws us from our flight?"
They asked, for spirits feel all force divine,
And know the sacred presence of the pure.
Then, looking downward, they beheld the Buddh
Crowned with a rose-hued aureole, intent
On thoughts to save; while from the grove a voice
Cried, "Rishis! this is He shall help the world,
Descend and worship." So the Bright Ones came
And sang a song of praise, folding their wings,
Then journeyed on, taking good news to Gods.

But certain from the King seeking the Prince
Found him still musing, though the noon was past,
And the sun hastened to the western hills
Yet, while all shadows moved, the jambu-tree's
Stayed in one quarter, overspreading him,
Lest the sloped rays should strike that sacred head;
And he who saw this sight heard a voice say,
Amid the blossoms of the rose-apple,
"Let be the King's son! till the shadow goes
Forth from his heart my shadow will not shift."

Book The Second

Now, when our Lord was come to eighteen years,
The King commanded that there should be built
Three stately houses, one of hewn square beams
With cedar lining, warm for winter days;
One of veined marbles, cool for summer heat;

And one of burned bricks, with blue tiles bedecked,
Pleasant at seed-time, when the champaks bud--
Subha, Suramma, Ramma, were their names.
Delicious gardens round about them bloomed,
Streams wandered wild and musky thickets stretched,
With many a bright pavilion and fair lawn
In midst of which Siddartha strayed at will,
Some new delight provided every hour;
And happy hours he knew, for life was rich,
With youthful blood at quickest; yet still came
The shadows of his meditation back,
As the lake's silver dulls with driving clouds.

Which the King marking, called his Ministers:
"Bethink ye, sirs I how the old Rishi spake,"
He said, "and what my dream-readers foretold.
This boy, more dear to me than mine heart's blood,
Shall be of universal dominance,
Trampling the neck of all his enemies,
A King of kings--and this is in my heart;--
Or he shall tread the sad and lowly path
Of self-denial and of pious pains,
Gaining who knows what good, when all is lost
Worth keeping; and to this his wistful eyes
Do still incline amid my palaces.
But ye are sage, and ye will counsel me;
How may his feet be turned to that proud road
Where they should walk, and all fair signs come true
Which gave him Earth to rule, if he would rule?"

The eldest answered, "Maharaja! love
Will cure these thin distempers; weave the spell
Of woman's wiles about his idle heart.
What knows this noble boy of beauty yet,
Eyes that make heaven forgot, and lips of balm?
Find him soft wives and pretty playfellows;

The Light Of Asia

The thoughts ye cannot stay with brazen chains
A girl's hair lightly binds."

And all thought good,
But the King answered, "if we seek him wives,
Love chooseth ofttimes with another eye;
And if we bid range Beauty's garden round,
To pluck what blossom pleases, he will smile
And sweetly shun the joy he knows not of."
Then said another, "Roams the barasingh
Until the fated arrow flies; for him,
As for less lordly spirits, some one charms,
Some face will seem a Paradise, some form
Fairer than pale Dawn when she wakes the world.
This do, my King! Command a festival
Where the realm's maids shall be competitors
In youth and grace, and sports that Sakyas use.
Let the Prince give the prizes to the fair,
And, when the lovely victors pass his seat,
There shall be those who mark if one or two
Change the fixed sadness of his tender cheek;
So we may choose for Love with Love's own eyes,
And cheat his Highness into happiness."
This thing seemed good; wherefore upon a day
The criers bade the young and beautiful
Pass to the palace, for 't was in command
To hold a court of pleasure, and the Prince
Would give the prizes, something rich for all,
The richest for the fairest judged. So flocked
Kapilavastu's maidens to the gate,
Each with her dark hair newly smoothed and bound,
Eyelashes lustred with the soorma-stick,
Fresh-bathed and scented; all in shawls and cloths
Of gayest; slender hands and feet new-stained
With crimson, and the tilka-spots stamped bright.
Fair show it was of all those Indian girls

    Slow-pacing past the throne with large black eyes
Fixed on the ground, for when they saw the Prince
    More than the awe of Majesty made beat
    Their fluttering hearts, he sate so passionless,
    Gentle, but so beyond them. Each maid took
    With down-dropped lids her gift, afraid to gaze;
    And if the people hailed some lovelier one
        Beyond her rivals worthy royal smiles,
    She stood like a scared antelope to touch
The gracious hand, then fled to join her mates
    Trembling at favour, so divine he seemed,
So high and saint-like and above her world.
Thus filed they, one bright maid after another,
The city's flowers, and all this beauteous march
    Was ending and the prizes spent, when last
    Came young Yasodhara, and they that stood
        Nearest Siddartha saw the princely boy
    Start, as the radiant girl approached. A form
    Of heavenly mould; a gait like Parvati's; the
    Eyes like a hind's in love-time, face so fair
Words cannot paint its spell; and she alone
Gazed full-folding her palms across her breasts
    On the boy's gaze, her stately neck unbent.
"Is there a gift for me?" she asked, and smiled.
"The gifts are gone," the Prince replied, "yet take
    This for amends, dear sister, of whose grace
    Our happy city boasts;" therewith he loosed
The emerald necklet from his throat, and clasped
Its green beads round her dark and silk-soft waist;
And their eyes mixed, and from the look sprang love.

        Long after--when enlightenment was full--
    Lord Buddha--being prayed why thus his heart
        Took fire at first glance of the Sakya girl,
        Answered, "We were not strangers, as to us
        And all it seemed; in ages long gone by

The Light Of Asia

A hunter's son, playing with forest girls
By Yamun's spring, where Nandadevi stands,
Sate umpire while they raced beneath the firs
Like hares at eve that run their playful rings;
One with flower-stars crowned he, one with long plumes
Plucked from eyed pheasant and the junglecock,
One with fir-apples; but who ran the last
Came first for him, and unto her the boy
Gave a tame fawn and his heart's love beside.
And in the wood they lived many glad years,
And in the wood they undivided died.
Lo! as hid seed shoots after rainless years,
So good and evil, pains and pleasures, hates
And loves, and all dead deeds, come forth again
Bearing bright leaves or dark, sweet fruit or sour.
Thus I was he and she Yasodhara;
And while the wheel of birth and death turns round,
That which hath been must be between us two."

But they who watched the Prince at prize-giving
Saw and heard all, and told the careful King
How sate Sidddrtha heedless till there passed
Great Suprabuddha's child, Yasodhara;
And how--at sudden sight of her--he changed,
And how she gazed on him and he on her,
And of the jewel-gift, and what beside
Passed in their speaking glance.

The fond King smiled:
"Look! we have found a lure; take counsel now
To fetch therewith our falcon from the clouds.
Let messengers be sent to ask the maid
In marriage for my son." But it was law
With Sakyas, when any asked a maid
Of noble house, fair and desirable,
He must make good his skill in martial arts

Against all suitors who should challenge it;
Nor might this custom break itself for kings.
Therefore her father spake: "Say to the King,
The child is sought by princes far and near;
If thy most gentle son can bend the bow,
Sway sword, and back a horse better than they,
Best would he be in all and best to us
But how shall this be, with his cloistered ways?"
Then the King's heart was sore, for now the Prince
Begged sweet Yasodhara for wife--in vain,
With Devadatta foremost at the bow,
Ardjuna master of all fiery steeds,
And Nanda chief in sword-play; but the Prince
Laughed low and said, "These things, too, I
have learned;
Make proclamation that thy son will meet
All comers at their chosen games. I think
I shall not lose my love for such as these."
So 't was given forth that on the seventh day
The Prince Siddartha summoned whoso would
To match with him in feats of manliness,
The victor's crown to be Yasodhara.

Therefore, upon the seventh day, there went
The Sakya lords and town and country round
Unto the maidan; and the maid went too
Amid her kinsfolk, carried as a bride,
With music, and with litters gaily dight,
And gold-horned oxen, flower-caparisoned.
Whom Devadatta claimed, of royal line,
And Nanda and Ardjuna, noble both,
The flower of all youths there, till the Prince came
Riding his white horse Kantaka, which neighed,
Astonished at this great strange world without
Also Siddartha gazed with wondering eyes
On all those people born beneath the throne,

The Light Of Asia

Otherwise housed than kings, otherwise fed,
And yet so like--perchance--in joys and griefs.
But when the Prince saw sweet Yasodhara,
Brightly he smiled, and drew his silken rein,
Leaped to the earth from Kantaka's broad back,
And cried, "He is not worthy of this pearl
Who is not worthiest; let my rivals prove
If I have dared too much in seeking her."
Then Nanda challenged for the arrow-test
And set a brazen drum six gows away,
Ardjuna six and Devadatta eight;
But Prince Siddartha bade them set his drum
Ten gows from off the line, until it seemed
A cowry-shell for target. Then they loosed,
And Nanda pierced his drum, Ardjuna his,
And Devadatta drove a well-aimed shaft
Through both sides of his mark, so that the crowd
Marvelled and cried; and sweet Yasodhara
Dropped the gold sari o'er her fearful eyes,
Lest she should see her Prince's arrow fail.
But he, taking their bow of lacquered cane,
With sinews bound, and strung with silver wire,
Which none but stalwart arms could draw a span,
Thrummed it--low laughing--drew the twisted string
Till the horns kissed, and the thick belly snapped
"That is for play, not love," he said; "hath none
A bow more fit for Sakya lords to use?"
And one said, "There is Sinhahanu's bow,
Kept in the temple since we know not when,
Which none can string, nor draw if it be strung."
"Fetch me," he cried, "that weapon of a man!"
They brought the ancient bow, wrought of black steel,
Laid with gold tendrils on its branching curves
Like bison-horns; and twice Siddartha tried
Its strength across his knee, then spake "Shoot now
With this, my cousins!" but they could not bring

The stubborn arms a hand's-breadth nigher use;
Then the Prince, lightly leaning, bent the bow,
Slipped home the eye upon the notch, and twanged
Sharply the cord, which, like an eagle's wing
Thrilling the air, sang forth so clear and loud
That feeble folk at home that day inquired
"What is this sound?" and people answered them,
"It is the sound of Sinhahanu's bow,
Which the King's son has strung and goes to shoot;"
Then fitting fair a shaft, he drew and loosed,
And the keen arrow clove the sky, and drave
Right through that farthest drum, nor stayed its flight,
But skimmed the plain beyond, past reach of eye.

Then Devadatta challenged with the sword,
And clove a Talas-tree six fingers thick;
Ardjuna seven; and Nanda cut through nine;
But two such stems together grew, and both
Siddartha's blade shred at one flashing stroke,
Keen, but so smooth that the straight trunks upstood,
And Nanda cried, "His edge turned!" and the maid
Trembled anew seeing the trees erect,
Until the Devas of the air, who watched,
Blew light breaths from the south, and both green crowns
Crashed in the sand, clean-felled.

Then brought they steeds,
High-mettled, nobly-bred, and three times scoured
Around the maidan, but white Kantaka
Left even the fleetest far behind--so swift,
That ere the foam fell from his mouth to earth
Twenty spear-lengths he flew; but Nanda said,
"We too might win with such as Kantaka;
Bring an unbroken horse, and let men see
Who best can back him." So the syces brought
A stallion dark as night, led by three chains,

The Light Of Asia

Fierce-eyed, with nostrils wide and tossing mane,
Unshod, unsaddled, for no rider yet
Had crossed him. Three times each young Sakya
Sprang to his mighty back, but the hot steed
Furiously reared, and flung them to the plain
In dust and shame; only Ardjuna held
His seat awhile, and, bidding loose the chains,
Lashed the black flank, and shook the bit, and held
The proud jaws fast with grasp of master-hand,
So that in storms of wrath and rage and fear
The savage stallion circled once the plain
Half-tamed; but sudden turned with naked teeth,
Gripped by the foot Ardjuna, tore him down,
And would have slain him, but the grooms ran in,
Fettering the maddened beast. Then all men cried,
"Let not Siddartha meddle with this Bhut,
Whose liver is a tempest, and his blood
Red flame;" but the Prince said, "Let go the chains,
Give me his forelock only," which he held
With quiet grasp, and, speaking some low word,
Laid his right palm across the stallion's eyes,
And drew it gently down the angry face,
And all along the neck and panting flanks,
Till men astonished saw the night-black horse
Sink his fierce crest and stand subdued and meek,
As though he knew our Lord and worshipped him.
Nor stirred he while Siddartha mounted, then
Went soberly to touch of knee and rein
Before all eyes, so that the people said,
"Strive no more, for Siddartha is the best."

And all the suitors answered "He is best!"
And Suprabuddha, father of the maid,
Said, "It was in our hearts to find thee best,
Being dearest, yet what magic taught thee more
Of manhood 'mid thy rose-bowers and thy dreams

Than war and chase and world's work bring to these?
But wear, fair Prince, the treasure thou halt won."
       Then at a word the lovely Indian girl
Rose from her place above the throng, and took
   A crown of mogra-flowers and lightly drew
   The veil of black and gold across her brow,
   Proud pacing past the youths, until she came
     To where Siddartha stood in grace divine,
New lighted from the night-dark steed, which bent
      Its strong neck meekly underneath his arm.
   Before the Prince lowly she bowed, and bared
       Her face celestial beaming with glad love;
    Then on his neck she hung the fragrant wreath,
    And on his breast she laid her perfect head,
And stooped to touch his feet with proud glad eyes,
     Saying, "Dear Prince, behold me, who am thine!"
       And all the throng rejoiced, seeing them pass
   Hand fast in hand, and heart beating with heart,
      The veil of black and gold drawn close again.

       Long after--when enlightenment was come--
     They prayed Lord Buddha touching all, and why
   She wore this black and gold, and stepped so proud.
       And the World-honoured answered, "Unto me
    This was unknown, albeit it seemed half known;
  For while the wheel of birth and death turns round,
 Past things and thoughts, and buried lives come back.
          I now remember, myriad rains ago,
      What time I roamed Himala's hanging woods,
         A tiger, with my striped and hungry kind;
      I, who am Buddh, couched in the kusa grass
   Gazing with green blinked eyes upon the herds
  Which pastured near and nearer to their death
     Round my day-lair; or underneath the stars
         I roamed for prey, savage, insatiable,
     Sniffing the paths for track of man and deer.

The Light Of Asia

Amid the beasts that were my fellows then,
Met in deep jungle or by reedy jheel,
A tigress, comeliest of the forest, set
The males at war; her hide was lit with gold,
Black-broidered like the veil Yasodhara
Wore for me; hot the strife waged in that wood
With tooth and claw, while underneath a neem
The fair beast watched us bleed, thus fiercely wooed.
And I remember, at the end she came
Snarling past this and that torn forest-lord
Which I had conquered, and with fawning jaws
Licked my quick-heaving flank, and with me went
Into the wild with proud steps, amorously.
The wheel of birth and death turns low and high."

Therefore the maid was given unto the Prince
A willing spoil; and when the stars were good--
Mesha, the Red Ram, being Lord of heaven--
The marriage feast was kept, as Sakyas use,
The golden gadi set, the carpet spread,
The wedding garlands hung, the arm-threads tied,
The sweet cake broke, the rice and attar thrown,
The two straws floated on the reddened milk,
Which, coming close, betokened "love till death;"
The seven steps taken thrice around the fire,
The gifts bestowed on holy men, the alms
And temple offerings made, the mantras sung,
The garments of the bride and bridegroom tied.
Then the grey father spake: "Worshipful Prince,
She that was ours henceforth is only thine;
Be good to her, who hath her life in thee."
Wherewith they brought home sweet Yasodhara,
With songs and trumpets, to the Prince's arms,
And love was all in all.

Yet not to love

Alone trusted the King; love's prison-house
Stately and beautiful he bade them build,
So that in all the earth no marvel was
Like Vishramvan, the Prince's pleasure-place.
Midway in those wide palace-grounds there rose
A verdant hill whose base Rohini bathed,
Murmuring adown from Himalay's broad feet,
To bear its tribute into Gunga's waves.
Southward a growth of tamarind trees and sal,
Thick set with pale sky-coloured ganthi flowers,
Shut out the world, save if the city's hum
Came on the wind no harsher than when bees
Hum out of sight in thickets. Northward soared
The stainless ramps of huge Hamala's wall,
Ranged in white ranks against the blue-untrod
Infinite, wonderful--whose uplands vast,
And lifted universe of crest and crag,
Shoulder and shelf, green slope and icy horn,
Riven ravine, and splintered precipice
Led climbing thought higher and higher, until
It seemed to stand in heaven and speak with gods.
Beneath the snows dark forests spread, sharp laced
With leaping cataracts and veiled with clouds
Lower grew rose-oaks and the great fir groves
Where echoed pheasant's call and panther's cry
Clatter of wild sheep on the stones, and scream
Of circling eagles: under these the plain
Gleamed like a praying-carpet at the foot
Of those divinest altars. 'Fronting this
The builders set the bright pavilion up,
'Fair-planted on the terraced hill, with towers
On either flank and pillared cloisters round.
Its beams were carved with stories of old time--
Radha and Krishna and the sylvan girls--
Sita and Hanuman and Draupadi;
And on the middle porch God Ganesha,

The Light Of Asia

With disc and hook--to bring wisdom and wealth--
Propitious sate, wreathing his sidelong trunk.
By winding ways of garden and of court
The inner gate was reached, of marble wrought,
White with pink veins; the lintel lazuli,
The threshold alabaster, and the doors
Sandalwood, cut in pictured panelling;
Whereby to lofty halls and shadowy bowers
Passed the delighted foot, on stately stairs,
Through latticed galleries, 'neath painted roofs
And clustering columns, where cool fountains--fringed
With lotus and nelumbo--danced, and fish
Gleamed through their crystal, scarlet, gold, and blue.
Great-eyed gazelles in sunny alcoves browsed
The blown red roses; birds of rainbow wing
Fluttered among the palms; doves, green and grey,
Built their safe nests on gilded cornices;
Over the shining pavements peacocks drew
The splendours of their trains, sedately watched
By milk-white herons and the small house-owls.
The plum-necked parrots swung from fruit to fruit;
The yellow sunbirds whirred from bloom to bloom,
The timid lizards on the lattice basked
Fearless, the squirrels ran to feed from hand,
For all was peace: the shy black snake, that gives
Fortune to households, sunned his sleepy coils
Under the moon-flowers, where the musk-deer played,
And brown-eyed monkeys chattered to the crows.
And all this house of love was peopled fair
With sweet attendance, so that in each part
With lovely sights were gentle faces found,
Soft speech and willing service, each one glad
To gladden, pleased at pleasure, proud to obey;
Till life glided beguiled, like a smooth stream
Banked by perpetual flowers, Yasodhara
Queen of the enchanting Court.

But innermost,
Beyond the richness of those hundred halls,
A secret chamber lurked, where skill had spent
All lovely fantasies to lull the mind.
The entrance of it was a cloistered square--
Roofed by the sky, and in the midst a tank--
Of milky marble built, and laid with slabs
Of milk-white marble; bordered round the tank
And on the steps, and all along the frieze
With tender inlaid work of agate-stones.
Cool as to tread in summer-time on snows
It was to loiter there; the sunbeams dropped
Their gold, and, passing into porch and niche,
Softened to shadows, silvery, pale, and dim,
As if the very Day paused and grew Eve.
In love and silence at that bower's gate;
For there beyond the gate the chamber was,
Beautiful, sweet; a wonder of the world!
Soft light from perfumed lamps through windows fell
Of nakre and stained stars of lucent film
On golden cloths outspread, and silken beds,
And heavy splendour of the purdah's fringe,
Lifted to take only the loveliest in.
Here, whether it was night or day none knew,
For always streamed that softened light, more bright
Than sunrise, but as tender as the eve's;
And always breathed sweet airs, more joy-giving
Than morning's, but as cool as midnight's breath;
And night and day lutes sighed, and night and day
Delicious foods were spread, and dewy fruits,
Sherbets new chilled with snows of Himalay,
And sweetmeats made of subtle daintiness,
With sweet tree-milk in its own ivory cup.
And night and day served there a chosen band
Of nautch girls, cup-bearers, and cymballers,
Delicate, dark-browed ministers of love,

The Light Of Asia

Who fanned the sleeping eyes of the happy Prince,
And when he waked, led back his thoughts to bliss
With music whispering through the blooms, and charm
Of amorous songs and dreamy dances, linked
By chime of ankle-bells and wave of arms
And silver vina-strings; while essences
Of musk and champak and the blue haze spread
From burning spices soothed his soul again
To drowse by sweet Yasodhara; and thus
Siddartha lived forgetting.

Furthermore,
The King commanded that within those walls
No mention should be made of death or age,
Sorrow, or pain, or sickness. If one drooped
In the lovely Court--her dark glance dim, her feet
Faint in the dance--the guiltless criminal
Passed forth an exile from that Paradise,
Lest he should see and suffer at her woe.
Bright-eyed intendants watched to execute
Sentence on such as spake of the harsh world
Without, where aches and plagues were, tears and fears,
And wail of mourners, and grim fume of pyres.
`T was treason if a thread of silver strayed
In tress of singing-girl or nautch-dancer;
And every dawn the dying rose was plucked,
The dead leaves hid, all evil sights removed
For said the King, "If he shall pass his youth
Far from such things as move to wistfulness,
And brooding on the empty eggs of thought,
The shadow of this fate, too vast for man,
May fade, belike, and I shall see him grow
To that great stature of fair sovereignty
When he shall rule all lands--if he will rule--
The King of kings and glory of his time."

Wherefore, around that pleasant prison house
Where love was gaoler and delights its bars,
But far removed from sight--the King bade build
A massive wall, and in the wall a gate
With brazen folding-doors, which but to roll
Back on their hinges asked a hundred arms;
Also the noise of that prodigious gate
Opening was heard full half a yojana.
And inside this another gate he made,
And yet within another--through the three
Must one pass if he quit that pleasure-house.
Three mighty gates there were, bolted and barred,
And over each was set a faithful watch;
And the King's order said, "Suffer no man
To pass the gates, though he should be the Prince
This on your lives--even though it be my son."

Book The Third

In which calm home of happy life and love
Ligged our Lord Buddha, knowing not of woe,
Nor want, nor pain, nor plague, nor age, nor death,
Save as when sleepers roam dim seas in dreams,
And land awearied on the shores of day,
Bringing strange merchandise from that black voyage.
Thus ofttimes when he lay with gentle head
Lulled on the dark breasts of Yasodhara,
Her fond hands fanning slow his sleeping lids,
He would start up and cry, "My world! Oh, world!
I hear! I know! I come!" And she would ask,
"What ails my Lord?" with large eyes terrorstruck;
For at such times the pity in his look

The Light Of Asia

Was awful, and his visage like a god's.
Then would he smile again to stay her tears,
And bid the vinas sound; but once they set
A stringed gourd on the sill, there where the wind
Could linger o'er its notes and play at will--
Wild music makes the wind on silver strings--
And those who lay around heard only that;
But Prince Siddartha heard the Devas play,
And to his ears they sang such words as these:--

We are the voices of the wandering wind,
Which moan for rest and rest can never find;
Lo! as the wind is so is mortal life,
A moan, a sigh, a sob, a storm, a strife.

Wherefore and whence we are ye cannot know,
Nor where life springs nor whither life doth go;
We are as ye are, ghosts from the inane,
What pleasure have we of our changeful pain?

What pleasure hast thou of thy changeless bliss?
Nay, if love lasted, there were joy in this;
But life's way is the wind's way, all these things
Are but brief voices breathed on shifting strings.

O Maya's son! because we roam the earth
Moan we upon these strings; we make no mirth,
So many woes we see in many lands,
So many streaming eyes and wringing hands.

Yet mock we while we wail, for, could they know,
This life they cling to is but empty show;
'Twere all as well to bid a cloud to stand,
Or hold a running river with the hand.

But thou that art to save, thine hour is nigh!

The sad world waileth in its misery,
The blind world stumbleth on its round of pain;
Rise, Maya's child! wake! slumber not again!

We are the voices of the wandering wind
Wander thou, too, O Prince, thy rest to find;
Leave love for love of lovers, for woe's sake
Quit state for sorrow, and deliverance make.

So sigh we, passing o'er the silver strings,
To thee who know'st not yet of earthly things;
So say we; mocking, as we pass away,
These lovely shadows wherewith thou dost play.

Thereafter it befell he sate at eve
Amid his beauteous Court, holding the hand
Of sweet Yasodhara, and some maid told--
With breaks of music when her rich voice dropped--
An ancient tale to speed the hour of dusk,
Of love, and of a magic horse, and lands
Wonderful, distant, where pale peoples dwelled
And where the sun at night sank into seas.
Then spake he, sighing, "Chitra brings me back.
The wind's song in the strings with that fair tale.
Give her, Yasodhara, thy pearl for thanks.
But thou, my pearl! is there so wide a world?
Is there a land which sees the great sun roll
Into the waves, and are there hearts like ours,
Countless, unknown, not happy--it may be--
Whom we might succour if we knew of them?
Ofttimes I marvel, as the Lord of day
Treads from the east his kingly road of gold,
Who first on the world's edge hath hailed his beam,
The children of the morning; oftentimes,
Even in thine arms and on thy breasts, bright wife,
Sore have I panted, at the sun's decline,

The Light Of Asia

To pass with him into that crimson west
And see the peoples of the evening.
There must be many we should love--how else?
Now have I in this hour an ache, at last,
Thy soft lips cannot kiss away: oh, girl!
O Chitra! you that know of fairyland!
Where tether they that swift steed of the tale?
My palace for one day upon his back,
To ride and ride and see the spread of the earth!
Nay, if I had yon callow vulture's plumes--
The carrion heir of wider realms than mine--
How would I stretch for topmost Himalay,
Light where the rose-gleam lingers on those snows,
And strain my gaze with searching what is round!
Why have I never seen and never sought?
Tell me what lies beyond our brazen gates."

Then one replied, "The city first, fair Prince!
The temples, and the gardens, and the groves,
And then the fields, and afterwards fresh fields,
With nullahs, maidans, jungle, koss on koss;
And next King Bimbasara's realm, and then
The vast flat world, with crores on crores of folk."
"Good," said Siddartha, "let the word be sent
That Channa yoke my chariot--at noon
Tomorrow I shall ride and see beyond."

Whereof they told the King: "Our Lord, thy son,
Wills that his chariot be yoked at noon,
That he may ride abroad and see mankind."

"Yea!" spake the careful King, "'tis time he see!
But let the criers go about and bid
My city deck itself, so there be met
No noisome sight; and let none blind or maimed,
None that is sick or stricken deep in years,

No leper, and no feeble folk come forth."
Therefore the stones were swept, and up and down
The water-carriers sprinkled all the streets
From spirting skins, the housewives scattered fresh
Red powder on their thresholds, strung new wreaths,
And trimmed the tulsi-bush before their doors.
The paintings on the walls were heightened up
With liberal brush, the trees set thick with flags,
The idols gilded; in the four-went ways
Suryadeva and the great gods shone
'Mid shrines of leaves; so that the city seemed
A capital of some enchanted land.
Also the criers passed, with drum and gong,
Proclaiming loudly, "Ho! all citizens,
The King commands that there be seen today
No evil sight: let no one blind or maimed,
None that is sick or stricken deep in years,
No leper, and no feeble folk go forth.
Let none, too, burn his dead nor bring them out
Till nightfall. Thus Suddhodana commands."

So all was comely and the houses trim
Throughout Kapilavastu, while the Prince
Came forth in painted car, which two steers drew,
Snow-white, with swinging dewlaps and huge humps
Wrinkled against the carved and lacquered yoke.
Goodly it was to mark the people's joy
Greeting their Prince; and glad. Siddartha waxed
At sight of all those liege and friendly folk
Bright-clad and laughing as if life were good.
"Fair is the world," he said, "it likes me well!
And light and kind these men that are not kings,
And sweet my sisters here, who toil and tend;
What have I done for these to make them thus?
Why, if I love them, should those children know?
I pray take up yon pretty Sakya boy

The Light Of Asia

Who flung us flowers, and let him ride with me.
How good it is to reign in realms like this!
How simple pleasure is, if these be pleased
Because I come abroad! How many things
I need not if such little households hold
Enough to make our city full of smiles!
Drive, Channa! through the gates, and let me see
More of this gracious world I have not known."

So passed they through the gates, a joyous crowd
Thronging about the wheels, whereof some ran
Before the oxen, throwing wreaths, some stroked
Their silken flanks, some brought them rice and cakes,
All crying, "Jai! jai! for our noble Prince!"
Thus all the path was kept with gladsome looks
And filled with fair sights--for the King's word was
That such should be--when midway in the road,
Slow tottering from the hovel where he hid,
Crept forth a wretch in rags, haggard and foul,
An old, old man, whose shrivelled skin, suntanned,
Clung like a beast's hide to his fleshless bones.
Bent was his back with load of many days,
His eyepits red with rust of ancient tears,
His dim orbs blear with rheum, his toothless jaws
Wagging with palsy and the fright to see
So many and such joy. One skinny hand
Clutched a worn staff to prop his quavering limbs,
And one was pressed upon the ridge of ribs
Whence came in gasps the heavy painful breath.
"Alms!" moaned he, "give, good people! for I die
Tomorrow or the next day!" then the cough
Choked him, but still he stretched his palm, and stood
Blinking, and groaning 'mid his spasms, "Alms!"
Then those around had wrenched his feeble feet
Aside, and thrust him from the road again,
Saying, "The Prince! dost see? get to thy lair!"

But that Siddartha cried, "Let be! let be!
Channa! what thing is this who seems a man,
Yet surely only seems, being so bowed,
So miserable, so horrible, so sad?
Are men born sometimes thus? What meaneth he
Moaning 'tomorrow or next day I die?'
Finds he no food that so his bones jut forth?
What woe hath happened to this piteous one?"
Then answer made the charioteer, "Sweet Prince!
This is no other than an aged man.
Some fourscore years ago his back was straight,
His eye bright, and his body goodly: now
The thievish years have sucked his sap away,
Pillaged his strength and filched his will and wit;
His lamp has lost its oil, the wick burns black;
What life he keeps is one poor lingering spark
Which flickers for the finish: such is age;
Why should your Highness heed?"
Then spake the Prince
"But shall this come to others, or to all,
Or is it rare that one should be as he?"
"Most noble," answered Channa, "even as he,
Will all these grow if they shall live so long."
"But," quoth the Prince, "if I shall live as long
Shall I be thus; and if Yasodhara
Live fourscore years, is this old age for her,
Jalini, little Hasta, Gautami,
And Gunga, and the others?" "Yea, great Sir!"
The charioteer replied. Then spake the Prince
"Turn back, and drive me to my house again!
I have seen that I did not think to see."

Which pondering, to his beauteous Court returned
Wistful Siddartha, sad of mien and mood;
Nor tasted he the white cakes nor the fruits
Spread for the evening feast, nor once looked up

The Light Of Asia

While the best palace-dancers strove to charm
Nor spake--save one sad thing--when wofully
    Yasodhara sank to his feet and wept,
Sighing, "Hath not my Lord comfort in me?"
"Ah, Sweet!" he said, "such comfort that my soul
    Aches, thinking it must end, for it will end,
    And we shall both grow old, Yasodhara!
Loveless, unlovely, weak, and old, and bowed.
Nay, though we locked up love and life with lips
    So close that night and day our breaths grew one
    Time would thrust in between to filch away
My passion and thy grace, as black Night steals
The rose-gleams from you peak, which fade to grey
    And are not seen to fade. This have I found,
    And all my heart is darkened with its dread,
    And all my heart is fixed to think how Love
Might save its sweetness from the slayer, Time,
Who makes men old." So through that night he sate
    Sleepless, uncomforted.

    And all that night
The King Suddhodana dreamed troublous dreams.
    The first fear of his vision was a flag
Broad, glorious, glistening with a golden sun,
    The mark of Indra; but a strong wind blew,
    Rending its folds divine, and dashing it
    Into the dust; whereat a concourse came
Of shadowy Ones, who took the spoiled silk up
    And bore it eastward from the city gates.
    The second fear was ten huge elephants,
With silver tusks and feet that shook the earth,
Trampling the southern road in mighty march;
    And he who sate upon the foremost beast
Was the King's son--the others followed him.
    The third fear of the vision was a car,
Shining with blinding light, which four steeds drew,

Snorting white smoke and champing fiery foam;
And in the car the Prince Siddhartha sate.
The fourth fear was a wheel which turned and turned,
With nave of burning gold and jewelled spokes,
And strange things written on the binding tire,
Which seemed both fire and music as it whirled.
The fifth fear was a mighty drum, set down
Midway between the city and the hills,
On which the Prince beat with an iron mace,
So that the sound pealed like a thunderstorm,
Rolling around the sky and far away.
The sixth fear was a tower, which rose and rose
High o'er the city till its stately head
Shone crowned with clouds, and on the top the Prince
Stood, scattering from both hands, this way and that,
Gems of most lovely light, as if it rained
Jacynths and rubies; and the whole world came,
Striving to seize those treasures as they fell
Towards the four quarters. But the seventh fear was
A noise of wailing, and behold six men
Who wept and gnashed their teeth, and laid their palms
Upon their mouths, walking disconsolate.

These seven fears made the vision of his sleep,
But none of all his wisest dream-readers
Could tell their meaning. Then the King was wroth,
Saying, "There cometh evil to my house,
And none of ye have wit to help me know
What the great gods portend sending me this."
So in the city men went sorrowful
Because the King had dreamed seven signs of fear
Which none could read; but to the gate there came
An aged man, in robe of deer-skin clad,
By guise a hermit, known to none; he cried,
"Bring me before the King, for I can read
The vision of his sleep"; who, when he heard

The Light Of Asia

The sevenfold mysteries of the midnight dream,
Bowed reverent and said: "O Maharaj!
I hail this favoured House, whence shall arise
A wider-reaching splendour than the sun's!
Lo! all these seven fears are seven joys,
Whereof the first, where thou didst see a flag--
Broad, glorious, gilt with Indra's badge--cast down
And carried out, did signify the end
Of old faiths and beginning of the new,
For there is change with gods not less than men,
And as the days pass kalpas pass at length.
The ten great elephants that shook the earth
The ten great gifts of wisdom signify,
In strength whereof the Prince shall quit his state
And shake the world with passage of the Truth.
The four flame-breathing horses of the car
Are those four fearless virtues which shall bring
Thy son from doubt and gloom to gladsome light;
The wheel that turned with nave of burning gold
Was that most precious Wheel of perfect Law
Which he shall turn in sight of all the world.
The mighty drum whereon the Prince did beat,
Till the sound filled all lands, doth signify
The thunder of the preaching of the Word
Which he shall preach; the tower that grew to heaven
The growing of the Gospel of this Buddh
Sets forth; and those rare jewels scattered thence
The untold treasures are of that good Law
To gods and men dear and desirable.
Such is the interpretation of the tower;
But for those six men weeping with shut mouths,
They are the six chief teachers whom thy son
Shall, with bright truth and speech unanswerable,
Convince of foolishness. O King! rejoice;
The fortune of my Lord the Prince is more
Than kingdoms, and his hermit-rags will be

Beyond fine cloths of gold. This was thy dream!
And in seven nights and days these things shall fall."
So spake the holy man, and lowly made
The eight prostrations, touching thrice the ground;
Then turned and passed; but when the King bade send

A rich gift after him, the messengers
Brought word, "We came to where he entered in
At Chandra's temple, but within was none
Save a grey owl which fluttered from the shrine."
The gods come sometimes thus.

But the sad King
Marvelled, and gave command that new delights
Be compassed to enthrall Siddartha's heart
Amid those dancers of his pleasure-house,
Also he set at all the brazen doors
A doubled guard.

Yet who shall shut out Fate?

For once again the spirit of the Prince
Was moved to see this world beyond his gates,
This life of man, so pleasant if its waves
Ran not to waste and woful finishing
In Time's dry sands. "I pray you let me view
Our city as it is," such was his prayer
To King Suddhodana. "Your Majesty
In tender heed hath warned the folk before
To put away ill things and common sights,
And make their faces glad to gladden me,
And all the causeways gay; yet have I learned
This is not daily life, and if I stand
Nearest, my father, to the realm and thee,
Fain would I know the people and the streets,
Their simple usual ways, and workday deeds,

The Light Of Asia

And lives which those men live who are not kings.
Give me good leave, dear Lord, to pass unknown
　　Beyond my happy gardens; I shall come
　　The more contented to their peace again,
　　　Or wiser, father, if not well content.
　　Therefore, I pray thee, let me go at will
Tomorrow, with my servants, through the streets."
　　And the King said, among his Ministers
"Belike this second flight may mend the first.
　　Note how the falcon starts at every sight
　　New from his hood, but what a quiet eye
　　Cometh of freedom; let my son see all,
　　And bid them bring me tidings of his mind."

　　Thus on the morrow, when the noon was come,
　　The Prince and Channa passed beyond the gates,
　　　Which opened to the signet of the King,
Yet knew not they who rolled the great doors back
　　It was the King's son in that merchant's robe,
　　　And in the clerkly dress his charioteer.
　　Forth fared they by the common way afoot,
　　　Mingling with all the Sakya citizens,
　　　Seeing the glad and sad things of the town:
　　The painted streets alive with hum of noon,
The traders cross-legged 'mid their spice and grain,
　　　The buyers with their money in the cloth,
　　The war of words to cheapen this or that,
The shout to clear the road, the huge stone wheels,
　　The strong slow oxen and their rustling loads,
　　　The singing bearers with the palanquins,
　　The broad-necked hamals sweating in the sun,
　　The housewives bearing water from the well
　　With balanced chatties, and athwart their hips
The black-eyed babes; the fly-swarmed sweetmeat shops,
　　　The weaver at his loom, the cotton-bow
Twangling, the millstones grinding meal, the dogs

Prowling for orts, the skilful armourer
With tong and hammer linking shirts of mail,
The blacksmith with a mattock and a spear
Reddening together in his coals, the school
Where round their Guru, in a grave half-moon,
The Sakya children sang the mantra through,
And learned the greater and the lesser gods;
The dyers stretching waistcloths in the sun
Wet from the vats--orange, and rose, and green;
The soldiers clanking past with swords and shields,
The camel-drivers rocking on the humps,
The Brahman proud, the martial Kshatriya,
The humble toiling Sudra; here a throng
Gathered to watch some chattering snake-tamer
Wind round his wrist the living jewellery
Of asp and nag, or charm the hooded death
To angry dance with drone of beaded gourd;
There a long line of drums and horns, which went,
With steeds gay painted and silk canopies,
To bring the young bride home; and here a wife
Stealing with cakes and garlands to the god
To pray her husband's safe return from trade,
Or beg a boy next birth; hard by the booths
Where the sweat potters beat the noisy brass
For lamps and lotas; thence, by temple walls
And gateways, to the river and the bridge
Under the city walls.

These had they passed
When from the roadside moaned a mournful voice,
"Help, masters! lift me to my feet; oh, help!
Or I shall die before I reach my house!"
A stricken wretch it was, whose quivering frame,
Caught by some deadly plague, lay in the dust
Writhing, with fiery purple blotches specked;
The chill sweat beaded on his brow, his mouth

The Light Of Asia

Was dragged awry with twichings of sore pain,
The wild eyes swam with inward agony.
Gasping, he clutched the grass to rise, and rose
Half-way, then sank, with quaking feeble limbs
And scream of terror, crying, "Ah, the pain!
Good people, help!" whereon Siddartha ran,
Lifted the woful man with tender hands,
With sweet looks laid the sick head on his knee,
And while his soft touch comforted the wretch,
Asked: "Brother, what is ill with thee? what harm
Hath fallen? wherefore canst thou not arise?
Why is it, Channa, that he pants and moans,
And gasps to speak and sighs so pitiful?"
Then spake the charioteer: "Great Prince! this man
Is smitten with some pest; his elements
Are all confounded; in his veins the blood,
Which ran a wholesome river, leaps and boils
A fiery flood; his heart, which kept good time,
Beats like an ill-played drum-skin, quick and slow;
His sinews slacken like a bow-string slipped;
The strength is gone from ham, and loin, and neck,
And all the grace and joy of manhood fled;
This is a sick man with the fit upon him.
See how be plucks and plucks to seize his grief,
And rolls his bloodshot orbs and grinds his teeth,
And draws his breath as if 'twere choking smoke.
Lo! now he would be dead, but shall not die
Until the plague hath had its work in him,
Killing the nerves which die before the life;
Then, when his strings have cracked with agony
And all his bones are empty of the sense
To ache, the plague will quit and light elsewhere.
Oh, sir! it is not good to hold him so!
The harm may pass, and strike thee, even thee."
But spake the Prince, still comforting the man,
"And are there others, are there many thus?

Or might it be to me as now with him?"
"Great Lord!" answered the charioteer, "this comes
In many forms to all men; griefs and wounds,
Sickness and tetters, palsies, leprosies,
Hot fevers, watery wastings, issues, blains
Befall all flesh and enter everywhere."
"Come such ills unobserved?" the Prince inquired.
And Channa said: "Like the sly snake they come
That stings unseen; like the striped murderer,
Who waits to spring from the Karunda bush,
Hiding beside the jungle path; or like
The lightning, striking these and sparing those,
As chance may send."

"Then all men live in fear?"
"So live they, Prince!"

"And none can say, 'I sleep
Happy and whole tonight, and so shall wake'?"
"None say it."

"And the end of many aches,
Which come unseen, and will come when they come,
Is this, a broken body and sad mind,
And so old age?"

"Yea, if men last as long."

"But if they cannot bear their agonies,
Or if they will not bear, and seek a term;
Or if they bear, and be, as this man is,
Too weak except for groans, and so still live,
And growing old, grow older, then what end?"

"They die, Prince."
"Die?"

The Light Of Asia

"Yea, at the last comes death,
In whatsoever way, whatever hour.
Some few grow old, most suffer and fall sick,
But all must die--behold, where comes the Dead!"

Then did Siddartha raise his eyes, and see
Fast pacing towards the river brink a band
Of wailing people, foremost one who swung
An earthen bowl with lighted coals, behind
The kinsmen shorn, with mourning marks, ungirt,
Crying aloud, "O Rama, Rama, hear!
Call upon Rama, brothers"; next the bier,
Knit of four poles with bamboos interlaced,
Whereon lay, stark and stiff, feet foremost, lean,
Chapfallen, sightless, hollow-flanked, a-grin,
Sprinkled with red and yellow dust--the Dead,
Whom at the four-went ways they turned head first,
And crying "Rama, Rama!" carried on
To where a pile was reared beside the stream;
Thereon they laid him, building fuel up--
Good sleep hath one that slumbers on that bed!
He shall not wake for cold albeit he lies
Naked to all the airs--for soon they set
The red flame to the corners four, which crept,
And licked, and flickered, finding out his flesh
And feeding on it with swift hissing tongues,
And crackle of parched skin, and snap of joint;
Till the fat smoke thinned and the ashes sank
Scarlet and grey, with here and there a bone
White midst the grey--the total of the man.

Then spake the Prince, "Is this the end which comes
To all who live?"

"This is the end that comes
To all," quoth Channa; "he upon the pyre--

Whose remnants are so petty that the crows
Caw hungrily, then quit the fruitless feast--
Ate, drank, laughed, loved, and lived, and liked
life well.
Then came--who knows?--some gust of junglewind,
A stumble on the path, a taint in the tank,
A snake's nip, half a span of angry steel,
A chill, a fishbone, or a falling tile,
And life was over and the man is dead.
No appetites, no pleasures, and no pains
Hath such; the kiss upon his lips is nought,
The fire-scorch nought; he smelleth not his flesh
A-roast, nor yet the sandal and the spice
They burn; the taste is emptied from his mouth,
The hearing of his ears is clogged, the sight
Is blinded in his eyes; those whom he loved
Wail desolate, for even that must go,
The body, which was lamp unto the life,
Or worms will have a horrid feast of it.
Here is the common destiny of flesh.
The high and low, the good and bad, must die,
And then, 't is taught, begin anew and live
Somewhere, somehow,--who knows?--and so again
The pangs, the parting, and the lighted pile--
Such is man's round."

But lo! Siddartha turned
Eyes gleaming with divine tears to the sky,
Eyes lit with heavenly pity to the earth;
From sky to earth he looked, from earth to sky,
As if his spirit sought in lonely flight
Some far-off vision, linking this and that,
Lost, past, but searchable, but seen, but known.
Then cried he, while his lifted countenance
Glowed with the burning passion of a love
Unspeakable, the ardour of a hope

The Light Of Asia

Boundless, insatiate: "Oh! suffering world,
Oh! known and unknown of my common flesh,
Caught in this common net of death and woe,
And life which binds to both! I see, I feel
The vastness of the agony of earth,
The vainness of its joys, the mockery
Of all its best, the anguish of its worst;
Since pleasures end in pain, and youth in age,
And love in loss, and life in hateful death,
And death in unknown lives, which will but yoke
Men to their wheel again to whirl the round
Of false delights and woes that are not false.
Me too this lure hath cheated, so it seemed
Lovely to live, and life a sunlit stream
For ever flowing in a changeless peace;
Whereas the foolish ripple of the flood
Dances so lightly down by bloom and lawn
Only to pour its crystal quicklier
Into the foul salt sea. The veil is rent
Which blinded me! I am as all these men
Who cry upon their gods and are not heard
Or are not heeded--yet there must be aid!
For them and me and all there must be help!
Perchance the gods have need of help themselves
Being so feeble that when sad lips cry
They cannot save! I would not let one cry
Whom I could save! How can it be that Brahm
Would make a world and keep it miserable,
Since, if all-powerful, he leaves it so,
He is not good, and if not powerful,
He is not God?--Channa! lead home again!
It is enough I mine eyes have seen enough!"

Which when the King heard, at the gates he set
A triple guard, and bade no man should pass
By day or night, issuing or entering in,

Until the days were numbered of that dream.

Book The Fourth

But when the days were numbered, then befell
The parting of our Lord--which was to be--
Whereby came wailing in the Golden Home,
Woe to the King and sorrow o'er the land,
But for all flesh deliverance, and that Law
Which whoso hears, the same shall make him free.

Softly the Indian night sinks on the plains
At full moon in the month of Chaitra Shud,
When mangoes redden and the asoka buds
Sweeten the breeze, and Rama's birthday comes,
And all the fields are glad and all the towns.
Softly that night fell over Vishramvan,
Fragrant with blooms and jewelled thick with stars,
And cool with mountain airs sighing adown
From snow-flats on Himala high-outspread;
For the moon swung above the eastern peaks,
Climbing the spangled vault, and lighting clear
Robini's ripples and the hills and plains,
And all the sleeping land, and near at hand
Silvering those roof-tops of the pleasure-house,
Where nothing stirred nor sign of watching was,
Save at the outer gates, whose warders cried
Mudra, the watchword, and the countersign
Angana, and the watch-drums beat a round;
Whereat the earth lay still, except for call
Of prowling jackals, and the ceaseless trill
Of crickets on the garden grounds.

The Light Of Asia

Within--
Where the moon glittered through the laceworked stone,
Lighting the walls of pearl-shell and the floors
Paved with veined marble--softly fell her beams
On such rare company of Indian girls,
It seemed some chamber sweet in Paradise
Where Devis rested. All the chosen ones
Of Prince Siddartha's pleasure-home were there,
The brightest and most faithful of the Court,
Each form so lovely in the peace of sleep,
That you had said "This is the pearl of all!"
Save that beside her or beyond her lay
Fairer and fairer, till the pleasured gaze
Roamed o'er that feast of beauty as it roams
From gem to gem in some great goldsmith-work,
Caught by each colour till the next is seen.
With careless grace they lay, their soft brown limbs
Part hidden, part revealed; their glossy hair
Bound back with gold or flowers, or flowing loose
In black waves down the shapely nape and neck.
Lulled into pleasant dreams by happy toils,
They slept, no wearier than jewelled birds
Which sing and love all day, then under wing
Fold head till morn bids sing and love again.
Lamps of chased silver swinging from the roof
In silver chains, and fed with perfumed oils,
Made with the moonbeams tender lights and shades,
Whereby were seen the perfect lines of grace,
The bosom's placid heave, the soft stained palms
Drooping or clasped, the faces fair and dark,
The great arched brows, the parted lips, the teeth
Like pearls a merchant picks to make a string,
The satin-lidded eyes, with lashes dropped
Sweeping the delicate cheeks, the rounded wrists
The smooth small feet with bells and bangles decked,
Tinkling low music where some sleeper moved,

Breaking her smiling dream of some new dance
Praised by the Prince, some magic ring to find,
Some fairy love-gift. Here one lay full-length,
Her vina by her cheek, and in its strings
The little fingers still all interlaced
As when the last notes of her light song played
Those radiant eyes to sleep and sealed her own.
Another slumbered folding in her arms
A desert-antelope, its slender head
Buried with back-sloped horns between her breasts
Soft nestling; it was eating--when both drowsed--
Red roses, and her loosening hand still held
A rose half-mumbled, while a rose-leaf curled
Between the deer's lips. Here two friends had dozed
Together, wearing mogra-buds, which bound
Their sister-sweetness in a starry chain,
Linking them limb to limb and heart to heart,
One pillowed on the blossoms, one on her.
Another, ere she slept, was stringing stones
To make a necklet--agate, onyx, sard,
Coral, and moonstone--round her wrist it gleamed
A coil of splendid colour, while she held,
Unthreaded yet, the bead to close it up
Green turkis, carved with golden gods and scripts.
Lulled by the cadence of the garden stream,
Thus lay they on the clustered carpets, each
A girlish rose with shut leaves, waiting dawn
To open and make daylight beautiful.
This was the antechamber of the Prince;
But at the purdah's fringe the sweetest slept--
Gunga and Gotami--chief ministers
In that still house of love.

The purdah hung,
Crimson and blue, with broidered threads of gold,
Across a portal carved in sandal-wood,

The Light Of Asia

Whence by three steps the way was to the bower
Of inmost splendour, and the marriage-couch
Set on a dais soft with silver cloths,
Where the foot fell as though it trod on piles
Of neem-blooms. All the walls, were plates of pearl,
Cut shapely from the shells of Lanka's wave;
And o'er the alabaster roof there ran
Rich inlayings of lotus and of bird,
Wrought in skilled work of lazulite and jade,
Jacynth and jasper; woven round the dome,
And down the sides, and all about the frames
Wherein were set the fretted lattices,
Through which there breathed, with moonlight and
cool airs,
Scents from the shell-flowers and the jasmine sprays;
Not bringing thither grace or tenderness
Sweeter than shed from those fair presences
Within the place--the beauteous Sakya Prince,
And hers, the stately, bright Yasodhara.

Half risen from her soft nest at his side,
The chuddah fallen to her waist, her brow
Laid in both palms, the lovely Princess leaned
With heaving bosom and fast falling tears.
Thrice with her lips she touched Siddartha's hand,
And at the third kiss moaned: "Awake, my Lord!
Give me the comfort of thy speech!" Then he--
"What is with thee, O my life?" but still
She moaned anew before the words would come;
Then spake: "'Alas, my Prince! I sank to sleep
Most happy, for the babe I bear of thee
Quickened this eve, and at my heart there beat
That double pulse of life and joy and love
Whose happy music lulled me, but--aho!--
In slumber I beheld three sights of dread,
With thought whereof my heart is throbbing yet.

I saw a white bull with wide branching horns,
A lord of pastures, pacing through the streets,
Bearing upon his front a gem which shone
As if some star had dropped to glitter there,
Or like the kantha-stone the great Snake keeps
To make bright daylight underneath the earth.
Slow through the streets toward the gates he paced,
And none could stay him, though there came a voice
From Indra's temple, 'If ye stay him not,
The glory of the city goeth forth.
Yet none could stay him. Then I wept aloud,
And locked my arms about his neck, and strove,
And bade them bar the gates; but that ox-king
Bellowed, and, lightly tossing free his crest,
Broke from my clasp, and bursting through the bars,
Trampled the warders down and passed away.
The neat strange dream was this: Four Presences
Splendid with shining eyes, so beautiful
They seemed the Regents of the Earth who dwell
On Mount Sumeru, lighting from the sky
With retinue of countless heavenly ones,
Swift swept unto our city, where I saw
The golden flag of Indra on the gate
Flutter and fall; and lo! there rose instead
A glorious banner, all the folds whereof
Rippled with flashing fire of rubies sewn
Thick on the silver threads, the rays wherefrom
Set forth new words and weighty sentences
Whose message made all living creatures glad;
And from the east the wind of sunrise blew
With tender waft, opening those jewelled scrolls
So that all flesh might read; and wondrous blooms
Plucked in what clime I know not-fell in showers,
Coloured as none are coloured in our groves."

Then spake the Prince: "All this, my Lotus-flower!

The Light Of Asia

Was good to see."

"Ay, Lord," the Princess said,
"Save that it ended with a voice of fear
Crying, 'The time is nigh! the time is nigh!'
Thereat the third dream came; for when I sought
Thy side, sweet Lord! ah, on our bed there lay
An unpressed pillow and an empty robe--
Nothing of thee but those!---nothing of thee,
Who art my life and light, my king, my world!
And sleeping still I rose, and sleeping saw
Thy belt of pearls, tied here below my breasts,
Change to a stinging snake; my ankle-rings
Fall off, my golden bangles part and fall;
The jasmines in my hair wither to dust;
While this our bridal-couch sank to the ground,
And something rent the crimson purdah down;
Then far away I heard the white bull low,
And far away the embroidered banner flap,
And once again that cry, 'The time is come!'
But with that cry--which shakes my spirit still--
I woke! O Prince! what may such visions mean
Except I die, or--worse than any death--
Thou shouldst forsake me or be taken?"

Sweet
As the last smile of sunset was the look
Siddartha bent upon his weeping wife.
"Comfort thee, dear!" he said, "if comfort lives
In changeless love; for though thy dreams may be
Shadows of things to come, and though the gods
Are shaken in their seats, and though the world
Stands nigh, perchance, to know some way of help,
Yet, whatsoever fall to thee and me,
Be sure I loved and love Yasodhara.
Thou knowest how I muse these many moons,

Seeking to save the sad earth I have seen;
And when the time comes, that which will be will.
But if my soul yearns sore for souls unknown,
And if I grieve for griefs which are not mine,
Judge how my high-winged thoughts must hover here
O'er all these lives that share and sweeten mine
So dear! and thine the dearest, gentlest, best,
And nearest. Ah, thou mother of my babe!
Whose body mixed with mine for this fair hope,
When most my spirit wanders, ranging round
The lands and seas--as full of ruth for men
As the far-flying dove is full of ruth
For her twin nestlings--ever it has come
Home with glad wing and passionate plumes to thee,
Who art the sweetness of my kind best seen,
The utmost of their good, the tenderest
Of all their tenderness, mine most of all.
Therefore, whatever after this betide,
Bethink thee of that lordly bull which lowed,
That jewelled banner in thy dreams which waved
Its folds departing, and of this be sure,
Always I loved and always love thee well,
And what I sought for all sought most for thee.
But thou, take comfort; and, if sorrow falls,
Take comfort still in deeming there may be
A way of peace on earth by woes of ours;
And have with this embrace what faithful love
Can think of thanks or frame for benison--
Too little, seeing love's strong self is weak--
Yet kiss me on the mouth, and drink these words
From heart to heart therewith, that thou mayst know--
What others will not--that I loved thee most
Because I loved so well all living souls.
Now, Princess! rest, for I will rise and watch."

Then in her tears she slept, but sleeping sighed--

The Light Of Asia

As if that vision passed again--"The time!
The time is come!" Whereat Siddartha turned,
And, lo! the moon shone by the Crab! the stars
　　In that same silver order long foretold
Stood ranged to say: "This is the night!--choose thou
　　The way of greatness or the way of good
　　To reign a King of kings, or wander lone,
Crownless and homeless, that the world be helped."
　　Moreover, with the whispers of the gloom
　　Came to his ears again that warning song,
　　As when the Devas spoke upon the wind:
　　And surely gods were round about the place
Watching our Lord, who watched the shining stars.

　　"I will depart," he spake; "the hour is come!
　　Thy tender lips, dear sleeper, summon me
　　To that which saves the earth but sunders us;
　　　　And in the silence of yon sky I read
　　　　My fated message flashing. Unto this
　　Came I, and unto this all nights and days
　　Have led me; for I will not have that crown
　　Which may be mine: I lay aside those realms
　　Which wait the gleaming of my naked sword
　　My chariot shall not roll with bloody wheels
　　　　From victory to victory, till earth
　　Wears the red record of my name. I choose
　　To tread its paths with patient, stainless feet,
　　Making its dust my bed, its loneliest wastes
My dwelling, and its meanest things my mates:
　　Clad in no prouder garb than outcasts wear,
　　Fed with no meats save what the charitable
　　Give of their will, sheltered by no more pomp
　　Than the dim cave lends or the jungle-bush,
　　　　This will I do because the woful cry
　　　　Of life and all flesh living cometh up
　　　　Into my ears, and all my soul is full

Of pity for the sickness of this world;
Which I will heal, if healing may be found
By uttermost renouncing and strong strife.
For which of all the great and lesser gods
Have power or pity? Who hath seen them--who?
What have they wrought to help their worshippers?
How hath it steaded man to pray, and pay
Tithes of the corn and oil, to chant the charms,
To slay the shrieking sacrifice, to rear
The stately fane, to feed the priests, and call
On Vishnu, Shiva, Surya, who save
None--not the worthiest--from the griefs that teach
Those litanies of flattery and fear
Ascending day by day, like wasted smoke?
Hath any of my brothers 'scaped thereby
The aches of life, the stings of love and loss,
The fiery fever and the ague-shake,
The slow, dull sinking into withered age,
The horrible dark death--and what beyond
Waits--till the whirling wheel comes up again,
And new lives bring new sorrows to be borne,
New generations for the new desires
Which have their end in the old mockeries?
Hath any of my tender sisters found
Fruit of the fast or harvest of the hymn,
Or bought one pang the less at bearing-time
For white curds offered and trim tulsi-leaves?
Nay; it may be some of the gods are good
And evil some, but all in action weak;
Both pitiful and pitiless, and both
As men are--bound upon this wheel of change,
Knowing the former and the after lives.
For so our scriptures truly seem to teach,
That--once, and wheresoe'er, and whence begun--
Life runs its rounds of living, climbing up
From mote, and gnat, and worm, reptile, and fish,

The Light Of Asia

Bird and shagged beast, man, demon, Deva, God,
To clod and mote again; so are we kin
To all that is; and thus, if one might save
Man from his curse, the whole wide world should share
The lightened horror of this ignorance
Whose shadow is chill fear, and cruelty
Its bitter pastime. Yea, if one might save!
And means must be! There must be refuge!"

"Men
Perished in winter-winds till one smote fire
From flint-stones coldly hiding what they held,
The red spark treasured from the kindling sun.
They gorged on flesh like wolves, till one sowed corn,
Which grew a weed, yet makes the life of man;
They mowed and babbled till some tongue struck speech,
And patient fingers framed the lettered sound.
What good gift have my brothers but it came
From search and strife and loving sacrifice?
If one, then, being great and fortunate,
Rich, dowered with health and ease, from birth designed
To rule--if he would rule--a King of kings;
If one, not tired with life's long day, but glad
I' the freshness of its morning, one not cloyed
With love's delicious feasts, but hungry still;
If one not worn and wrinkled, sadly sage,
But joyous in the glory and the grace
That mix with evils here, and free to choose
Earth's loveliest at his will: one even as I,
Who ache not, lack not, grieve not, save with griefs
Which are not mine, except as I am man;--
If such a one, having so much to give,
Gave all, laying it down for love of men.
And thenceforth spent himself to search for truth,
Wringing the secret of deliverance forth,
Whether it lurk in hells or hide in heavens,

Or hover, unrevealed, nigh unto all:
Surely at last, far off, sometime, somewhere,
The veil would lift for his deep-searching eyes,
The road would open for his painful feet,
That should be won for which he lost the world,
And Death might find him conqueror of death.
This will I do, who have a realm to lose,
Because I love my realm, because my heart
Beats with each throb of all the hearts that ache,
Known and unknown, these that are mine and those
Which shall be mine, a thousand million more
Saved by this sacrifice I offer now.
Oh, summoning stars! Oh, mournful earth
For thee and thine I lay aside my youth,
My throne, my joys, my golden days, my nights,
My happy palace--and thine arms, sweet Queen!
Harder to put aside than all the rest!
Yet thee, too, I shall save, saving this earth;
And that which stirs within thy tender womb,
My child, the hidden blossom of our loves,
Whom if I wait to bless my mind will fail.
Wife! child! father! and people! ye must share
A little while the anguish of this hour
That light may break and all flesh learn the Law.
Now am I fixed, and now I will depart,
Never to come again till what I seek
Be found--if fervent search and strife avail."

So with his brow he touched her feet, and bent
The farewell of fond eyes, unutterable,
Upon her sleeping face, still wet with tears;
And thrice around the bed in reverence,
As though it were an altar, softly stepped
With clasped hands laid upon his beating heart,
"For never," spake he, "lie I there again!"
And thrice he made to go, but thrice came back,

The Light Of Asia

So strong her beauty was, so large his love
Then, o'er his head drawing his cloth, he turned
And raised the purdah's edge.

There drooped, close-hushed,
In such sealed sleep as water-lilies know,
The lovely garden of his Indian girls;
Those twin dark-petalled lotus-buds of all--
Gunga and Gotami--on either side,
And those, their silk-leaved sisterhood, beyond.
"Pleasant ye are to me, sweet friends!" he said,
"And dear to leave; yet if I leave ye not
What else will come to all of us save eld
Without assuage and death without avail?
Lo! as ye lie asleep so must ye lie
A-dead; and when the rose dies where are gone
Its scent and splendour? when the lamp is drained
Whither is fled the flame? Press heavy, Night!
Upon their down-dropped lids and seal their lips,
That no tear stay me and no faithful voice.
For all the brighter that these made my life,
The bitterer it is that they and I,
And all, should live as trees do--so much spring,
Such and such rains and frosts, such wintertimes,
And then dead leaves, with maybe spring again,
Or axe-stroke at the root. This will not I,
Whose life here was a god's!--this would not I,
Though all my days were godlike, while men moan
Under their darkness. Therefore farewell, friends!
While life is good to give, I give, and go
To seek deliverance and that unknown Light!"

Then, lightly treading where those sleepers lay,
Into the night Siddartha passed: its eyes,
The watchful stars, looked love on him: its breath,
The wandering wind, kissed his robe's fluttered fringe;

The garden-blossoms, folded for the dawn,
Opened their velvet hearts to waft him scents
From pink and purple censers: o'er the land,
From Himalay unto the Indian Sea,
A tremor spread, as if earth's soul beneath
Stirred with an unknown hope; and holy books--
Which tell the story of our Lord--say, too,
That rich celestial musics thrilled the air
From hosts on hosts of shining ones, who thronged
Eastward and westward, making bright the night
Northward and southward, making glad the ground.
Also those four dread Regents of the Earth,
Descending at the doorway, two by two,--
With their bright legions of Invisibles
In arms of sapphire, silver, gold, and pearl--
Watched with joined hands the Indian Prince, who stood,
His tearful eyes raised to the stars, and lips
Close-set with purpose of prodigious love.

Then strode he forth into the gloom and cried,
"Channa, awake! and bring out Kantaka!"

"What would my Lord?" the charioteer replied--
Slow-rising from his place beside the gate
"To ride at night when all the ways are dark?"

"Speak low," Siddartha said, "and bring my horse,
For now the hour is come when I should quit
This golden prison where my heart lives caged
To find the truth; which henceforth I will seek,
For all men's sake, until the truth be found."

"Alas! dear Prince," answered the charioteer,
"Spake then for nought those wise and holy men
Who cast the stars and bade us wait the time
When King Suddhodana's great son should rule

The Light Of Asia

Realms upon realms, and be a Lord of lords?
Wilt thou ride hence and let the rich world slip
  Out of thy grasp, to hold a beggar's bowl?
  Wilt thou go forth into the friendless waste
  That hast this Paradise of pleasures here?"

The Prince made answer: "Unto this I came,
And not for thrones: the kingdom that I crave
Is more than many realms, and all things pass
To change and death. Bring me forth Kantaka!"

"Most honored," spake again the charioteer,

"Bethink thee of their woe whose bliss thou art--
How shalt thou help them, first undoing them?"

Siddartha answered: "Friend, that love is false
Which clings to love for selfish sweets of love;
But I, who love these more than joys of mine--
Yea, more than joy of theirs--depart to save
  Them and all flesh, if utmost love avail.
    Go, bring me Kantaka!"

        Then Channa said,
"Master, I go!" and forthwith, mournfully,
Unto the stall he passed, and from the rack
Took down the silver bit and bridle-chains,
Breast-cord and curb, and knitted fast the straps,
  And linked the hooks, and led out Kantaka
Whom tethering to the ring, he combed and dressed,
    Stroking the snowy coat to silken gloss;
    Next on the steed he laid the numdah square,
      Fitted the saddle-cloth across, and set
The saddle fair, drew tight the jewelled girths,
Buckled the breech-bands and the martingale,
And made fall both the stirrups of worked gold.

Then over all he cast a golden net,
With tassels of seed-pearl and silken strings,
And led the great horse to the palace door,
Where stood the Prince; but when he saw his Lord,
Right glad he waxed and joyously he neighed,
Spreading his scarlet nostrils; and the books
Write, "Surely all had heard Kantaka's neigh,
And that strong trampling of his iron heels,
Save that the Devas laid their unseen wings
Over their ears and kept the sleepers deaf."

Fondly Siddartha drew the proud head down,
Patted the shining neck, and said, "Be still,
White Kantaka! be still, and bear me now
The farthest journey ever rider rode;
For this night take I horse to find the truth,
And where my quest will end yet know I not,
Save that it shall not end until I find.
Therefore tonight, good steed, be fierce and bold!
Let nothing stay thee, though a thousand blades
Deny the road! let neither wall nor moat
Forbid our flight! Look! if I touch thy flank
And cry, 'On, Kantaka! I let whirlwinds lag
Behind thy course! Be fire and air, my horse!
To stead thy Lord, so shalt thou share with him
The greatness of this deed which helps the world;
For therefore ride I, not for men alone,
But for all things which, speechless, share our pain
And have no hope, nor wit to ask for hope.
Now, therefore, bear thy master valorously!"

Then to the saddle lightly leaping, he
Touched the arched crest, and Kantaka sprang forth
With armed hoofs sparkling on the stones and ring
Of champing bit; but none did hear that sound,
For that the Suddha Devas, gathering near,

The Light Of Asia

Plucked the red mohra-flowers and strewed them thick
Under his tread, while hands invisible
Muffled the ringing bit and bridle chains.
Moreover, it is written when they came
Upon the pavement near the inner gates,
The Yakshas of the air laid magic cloths
Under the stallion's feet, so that he went
Softly and still.

But when they reached the gate
Of tripled brass--which hardly fivescore men
Served to unbar and open--lo! the doors
Rolled back all silently, though one might hear
In daytime two koss off the thunderous roar
Of those grim hinges and unwieldy plates.

Also the middle and the outer gates
Unfolded each their monstrous portals thus
In silence as Siddartha and his steed
Drew near; while underneath their shadow lay.
Silent as dead men, all those chosen guards--
The lance and sword let fall, the shields unbraced,
Captains and soldiers--for there came a wind,
Drowsier than blows o'er Malwa's fields of sleep
Before the Prince's path, which, being breathed,
Lulled every sense aswoon: and so he passed
Free from the palace.

When the morning star
Stood half a spear's length from the eastern rim,
And o'er the earth the breath of morning sighed
Rippling Anoma's wave, the border-stream,
Then drew he rein, and leaped to earth and kissed
White Kantaka betwixt the ears, and spake
Full sweet to Channa: "This which thou hast done
Shall bring thee good and bring all creatures good.

Be sure I love thee always for thy love.
Lead back my horse and take my crest-pearl here,
My princely robes, which henceforth stead me not,
My jewelled sword-belt and my sword, and these
The long locks by its bright edge severed thus
From off my brows. Give the King all, and say
Siddartha prays forget him till he come
Ten times a prince, with royal wisdom won
From lonely searchings and the strife for light;
Where, if I conquer, lo! all earth is mine--
Mine by chief service!--tell him--mine by love!
Since there is hope for man only in man,
And none hath sought for this as I will seek,
Who cast away my world to save my world."

Book the Fifth

Round Rajagriha five fair hills arose,
Guarding King Bimbasara's sylvan town;
Baibhara, green with lemon-grass and palms;
Bipulla, at whose foot thin Sarsuti
Steals with warm ripple; shadowy Tapovan,
Whose steaming pools mirror black rocks, which ooze
Sovereign earth-butter from their rugged roofs;
South-east the vulture-peak Sailagiri;
And eastward Ratnagiri, hill of gems.
A winding track, paven with footworn slabs,
Leads thee by safflower fields and bamboo tufts
Under dark mangoes and the jujube-trees,
Past milk-white veins of rock and jasper crags,
Low cliff and flats of jungle-flowers, to where

The Light Of Asia

The shoulder of that mountain, sloping west,
O'erhangs a cave with wild figs canopied.
Lo! thou who comest thither, bare thy feet
And bow thy head! for all this spacious earth
Hath not a spot more dear and hallowed.
Here Lord Buddha sate the scorching summers through,
The driving rains, the chilly dawns and eves;
Wearing for all men's sakes the yellow robe,
Eating in beggar's guise the scanty meal
Chance-gathered from the charitable; at night
Crouched on the grass, homeless, alone; while yelped
The sleepless jackals round his cave, or coughs
Of famished tiger from the thicket broke.
By day and night here dwelt the World-honoured,
Subduing that fair body born for bliss
With fast and frequent watch and search intense
Of silent meditation, so prolonged
That ofttimes while he mused--as motionless
As the fixed rock his seat--the squirrel leaped
Upon his knee, the timid quail led forth
Her brood between his feet, and blue doves pecked
The rice-grains from the bowl beside his hand.

Thus would he muse from noontide--when the land
Shimmered with heat, and walls and temples danced
In the reeking air--till sunset, noting not
The blazing globe roll down, nor evening glide,
Purple and swift, across the softened fields;
Nor the still coming of the stars, nor throb
Of drum-skins in the busy town, nor screech
Of owl and night jar; wholly wrapt from self
In keen unraveling of the threads of thought
And steadfast pacing of life's labyrinths.
Thus would he sit till midnight hushed the world,
Save where the beasts of darkness in the brake
Crept and cried out, as fear and hatred cry,

As lust and avarice and anger creep
In the black jungles of man's ignorance.
Then slept he for what space the fleet moon asks
To swim a tenth part of her cloudy sea;
But rose ere the false-dawn, and stood again
Wistful on some dark platform of his hill,
Watching the sleeping earth with ardent eyes
And thoughts embracing all its living things,
While o'er the waving fields that murmur moved
Which is the kiss of Morn waking the lands,
And in the east that miracle of Day
Gathered and grew: at first a dusk so dim
Night seems still unaware of whispered dawn,
But soon--before the jungle-cock crows twice--
A white verge clear, a widening, brightening white,
High as the herald-star, which fades in floods
Of silver, warming into pale gold, caught
By topmost clouds, and flaming on their rims
To fervent golden glow, flushed from the brink
With saffron, scarlet, crimson, amethyst;
Whereat the sky burns splendid to the blue,
And, robed in raiment of glad light, the
Song Of Life and Glory cometh!

Then our Lord,
After the manner of a Rishi, hailed
The rising orb, and went--ablutions made--
Down by the winding path unto the town;
And in the fashion of a Rishi passed
From street to street, with begging-bowl in hand,
Gathering the little pittance of his needs.
Soon was it filled, for all the townsmen cried,
"Take of our store, great sir!" and "Take of ours!"
Marking his godlike face and eyes enwrapt;
And mothers, when they saw our Lord go by,
Would bid their children fall to kiss his feet,

The Light Of Asia

And lift his robe's hem to their brows, or run
To fill his jar, and fetch him milk and cakes.
And ofttimes as he paced, gentle and slow,
Radiant with heavenly pity, lost in care
For those he knew not, save as fellow lives,
The dark surprised eyes of some Indian maid
Would dwell in sudden love and worship deep
On that majestic form, as if she saw
Her dreams of tenderest thought made true, and grace
Fairer than mortal fire her breast. But he
Passed onward with the bowl and yellow robe,
By mild speech paying all those gifts of hearts,
Wending his way back to the solitudes
To sit upon his hill with holy men,
And hear and ask of wisdom and its roads.

Midway on Ratnagiri's groves of calm,
Beyond the city, but below the caves,
Lodged such as hold the body foe to soul,
And flesh a beast which men must chain and tame
With bitter pains, till sense of pain is killed,
And tortured nerves vex torturer no more--
Yogis and Brahmacharis, Bhikshus, all--
A gaunt and mournful band, dwelling apart.
Some day and night had stood with lifted arms,
Till--drained of blood and withered by disease
Their slowly-wasting joints and stiffened limbs
Jutted from sapless shoulders like dead forks
from forest trunks.
Others had clenched their hands
So long and with so fierce a fortitude,
The claw-like nails grew through the festered palm.
Some walked on sandals spiked; some with sharp flints
Gashed breast and brow and thigh, scarred these
with fire,
Threaded their flesh with jungle thorns and spits,

Besmeared with mud and ashes, crouching foul
In rags of dead men wrapped about their loins.
Certain there were inhabited the spots
Where death pyres smouldered, cowering defiled
With corpses for their company, and kites
Screaming around them o'er the funeral-spoils;
Certain who cried five hundred times a day
The names of Shiva, wound with darting snakes
About their sun-tanned necks and hollow flanks,
One palsied foot drawn up against the ham.
So gathered they, a grievous company;
Crowns blistered by the blazing heat, eyes bleared,
Sinews and muscles shrivelled, visages
Haggard and wan as slain men's, five days dead;
Here crouched one in the dust who noon by noon
Meted a thousand grains of millet out,
Ate it with famished patience, seed by seed,
And so starved on; there one who bruised his pulse
With bitter leaves lest palate should be pleased;
And next, a miserable saint self-maimed,
Eyeless and tongueless, sexless, crippled, deaf;
The body by the mind being thus stripped
For glory of much suffering, and the bliss
Which they shall win--say holy books--whose woe
Shames gods that send us woe, and makes men gods
Stronger to suffer than hell is to harm.

Whom sadly eyeing spake our Lord to one,
Chief of the woe-begones: "Much-suffering sir
These many moons I dwell upon the hill--
Who am a seeker of the Truth--and see
My brothers here, and thee, so piteously
Self-anguished; wherefore add ye ills to life
Which is so evil?"

Answer made the sage

The Light Of Asia

"'T is written if a man shall mortify
His flesh, till pain be grown the life he lives
And death voluptuous rest, such woes shall purge
Sin's dross away, and the soul, purified,
Soar from the furnace of its sorrow, winged
For glorious spheres and splendour past all thought."

"Yon cloud which floats in heaven," the Prince replied,
"Wreathed like gold cloth around your Indra's throne,
Rose thither from the tempest-driven sea;
But it must fall again in tearful drops,
Trickling through rough and painful water-ways
By cleft and nullah and the muddy flood,
To Gunga and the sea, wherefrom it sprang.
Know'st thou, my brother, if it be not thus,
After their many pains, with saints in bliss?
Since that which rises falls, and that which buys
Is spent; and if ye buy heaven with your blood
In hell's hard market, when the bargain's through
The toil begins again!"

"It may begin,"
The hermit moaned. "Alas! we know not this,
Nor surely anything; yet after night
Day comes, and after turmoil peace, and we
Hate this accursed flesh which clogs the soul
That fain would rise; so, for the sake of soul,
We stake brief agonies in game with Gods
To gain the larger joys."

"Yet if they last
A myriad years," he said, "they fade at length,
Those joys; or if not, is there then some life
Below, above, beyond, so unlike life it will not change?
Speak! do your Gods endure
For ever, brothers?"

"Nay," the Yogis said,
"Only great Brahm endures: the Gods but live."

Then spake Lord Buddha: "Will ye, being wise,
As ye seem holy and strong-hearted ones,
Throw these sore dice, which are your groans and moans,
For gains which may be dreams, and must have end?
Will ye, for love of soul, so loathe your flesh,
So scourge and maim it, that it shall not serve
To bear the spirit on, searching for home,
But founder on the track before nightfall,
Like willing steed o'er-spurred? Will ye, sad sirs,
Dismantle and dismember this fair house,
Where we have come to dwell by painful pasts;
Whose windows give us light--the little light
Whereby we gaze abroad to know if dawn
Will break, and whither winds the better road?"

Then cried they, "We have chosen this for road
And tread it, Rajaputra, till the close--
Though all its stones were fire--in trust of death.
Speak, if thou know'st a way more excellent;
If not, peace go with thee!"

Onward he passed,
Exceeding sorrowful, seeing how men
Fear so to die they are afraid to fear,
Lust so to live they dare not love their life,
But plague it with fierce penances, belike
To please the Gods who grudge pleasure to man;
Belike to balk hell by self-kindled hells;
Belike in holy madness, hoping soul
May break the better through their wasted flesh.
"Oh, flowerets of the field!" Siddartha said,
"Who turn your tender faces to the sun--

The Light Of Asia

Glad of the light, and grateful with sweet breath
Of fragrance and these robes of reverence donned
   Silver and gold and purple--none of ye
   Miss perfect living, none of ye despoil
  Your happy beauty. O, ye palms, which rise
   Eager to pierce the sky and drink the wind
  Blown from Malaya and the cool blue seas,
  What secret know ye that ye grow content,
  From time of tender shoot to time of fruit,
Murmuring such sun-songs from your feathered crowns?
   Ye, too, who dwell so merry in the trees--
Quick-darting parrots, bee-birds, bulbuls, doves--
   None of ye hate your life, none of ye deem
   To strain to better by foregoing needs!
  But man, who slays ye--being lord--is wise,
  And wisdom, nursed on blood, cometh thus forth
    In self-tormentings!"

         While the Master spake
Blew down the mount the dust of pattering feet,
White goats and black sheep winding slow their way,
   With many a lingering nibble at the tufts,
And wanderings from the path, where water gleamed
   Or wild figs hung. But always as they strayed
  The herdsman cried, or slung his sling, and kept
   The silly crowd still moving to the plain.
   A ewe with couplets in the flock there was.
Some hurt had lamed one lamb, which toiled behind
   Bleeding, while in the front its fellow skipped,
  And the vexed dam hither and thither ran,
   Fearful to lose this little one or that;
  Which when our Lord did mark, full tenderly
   He took the limping lamb upon his neck,
  Saying: "Poor woolly mother, be at peace!
   Whither thou goest I will bear thy care;
'T were all as good to ease one beast of grief

      As sit and watch the sorrows of the world
        In yonder caverns with the priests who pray."

"But," spake he to the herdsmen, "wherefore, friends,
    Drive ye the flocks adown under high noon,
    Since 't is at evening that men fold their sheep?"

    And answer gave the peasants: "We are sent
      To fetch a sacrifice of goats five score,
And five score sheep, the which our Lord the King
    Slayeth this night in worship of his gods."

      Then said the Master, "I will also go."
    So paced he patiently, bearing the lamb
    Beside the herdsmen in the dust and sun,
    The wistful ewe low-bleating at his feet.

    Whom, when they came unto the river-side,
A woman--dove-eyed, young, with tearful face
    And lifted hands--saluted, bending low
"Lord! thou art he," she said, "who yesterday
      Had pity on me in the fig-grove here,
Where I live lone and reared my child; but he
    Straying amid the blossoms found a snake,
Which twined about his wrist, while he did laugh
And tease the quick forked tongue and opened mouth
    Of that cold playmate. But, alas! ere long
He turned so pale and still, I could not think
    Why he should cease to play, and let my breast
    Fall from his lips. And one said, 'He is sick
      Of poison'; and another, 'He will die.'
    But I, who could not lose my precious boy,
Prayed of them physic, which might bring the light
    Back to his eyes; it was so very small
    That kiss-mark of the serpent, and I think
    It could not hate him, gracious as he was,

The Light Of Asia

Nor hurt him in his sport. And some one said,
'There is a holy man upon the hill
Lo! now he passeth in the yellow robe
Ask of the Rishi if there be a cure
For that which ails thy son.' Whereon I came
Trembling to thee, whose brow is like a god's,
And wept and drew the face cloth from my babe,
Praying thee tell what simples might be good.
And thou, great sir, did'st spurn me not, but gaze
With gentle eyes and touch with patient hand;
Then draw the face cloth back, saying to me,
'Yea, little sister, there is that might heal
Thee first, and him, if thou couldst fetch the thing;
For they who seek physicians bring to them
What is ordained. Therefore, I pray thee, find
Black mustard-seed, a tola; only mark
Thou take it not from any hand or house
Where father, mother, child, or slave hath died;
It shall be well if thou canst find such seed.'
Thus didst thou speak, my Lord!"

The Master smiled
Exceeding tenderly. "Yea, I spake thus,
Dear Kisagotami! But didst thou find The seed?"

"I went, Lord, clasping to my breast
The babe, grown colder, asking at each hut--
Here in the jungle and towards the town--
'I pray you, give me mustard, of your grace,
A tola-black'; and each who had it gave,
For all the poor are piteous to the poor;
But when I asked, 'In my friend's household here
Hath any peradventure ever died
Husband or wife, or child, or slave?' they said:
'O sister! what is this you ask? the dead
Are very many, and the living few!'

So with sad thanks I gave the mustard back,
And prayed of others; but the others said,
Here is the seed, but we have lost our slave.'
'Here is the seed, but our good man is dead!'
'Here is some seed, but he that sowed it died
Between the rain-time and the harvesting!'
Ah, sir! I could not find a single house
Where there was mustard-seed and none had died!
Therefore I left my child--who would not suck
Nor smile--beneath the wild vines by the stream,
To seek thy face and kiss thy feet, and pray
Where I might find this seed and find no death,
If now, indeed, my baby be not dead,
As I do fear, and as they said to me."

"My sister! thou hast found," the Master said,
"Searching for what none finds--that bitter balm
I had to give thee. He thou lovest slept
Dead on thy bosom yesterday: today
Thou know'st the whole wide world weeps with thy woe
The grief which all hearts share grows less for one.
Lo! I would pour my blood if it could stay
Thy tears and win the secret of that curse
Which makes sweet love our anguish, and which drives
O'er flowers and pastures to the sacrifice
As these dumb beasts are driven--men their lords.
I seek that secret: bury thou thy child!"

So entered they the city side by side,
The herdsmen and the Prince, what time the sun
Gilded slow Sona's distant stream, and threw
Long shadows down the street and through the gate
Where the King's men kept watch. But when they saw
Our Lord bearing the lamb, the guards stood back,
The market-people drew their wains aside,
In the bazaar buyers and sellers stayed

The Light Of Asia

The war of tongues to gaze on that mild face;
The smith, with lifted hammer in his hand,
Forgot to strike; the weaver left his web,
The scribe his scroll, the money-changer lost
His count of cowries; from the unwatched rice
Shiva's white bull fed free; the wasted milk
Ran o'er the lota while the milkers watched
The passage of our Lord moving so meek,
With yet so beautiful a majesty.
But most the women gathering in the doors
Asked: "Who is this that brings the sacrifice,
So graceful and peace-giving as he goes?
What is his caste? whence hath he eyes so sweet?
Can he be Sakra or the Devaraj?"
And others said, "It is the holy man
Who dwelleth with the Rishis on the hill."
But the Lord paced, in meditation lost,
Thinking, "Alas! for all my sheep which have
No shepherd; wandering in the night with none
To guide them; bleating blindly towards the knife
Of Death, as these dumb beasts which are their kin."

Then some one told the King, "There cometh here
A holy hermit, bringing down the flock
Which thou didst bid to crown the sacrifice."

The King stood in his hall of offering.
On either hand, the white-robed Brahmans ranged
Muttered their mantras, feeding still the fire
Which roared upon the midmost altar. There
From scented woods flickered bright tongues of flame,
Hissing and curling as they licked the gifts
Of ghee and spices and the soma juice,
The joy of Iudra. Round about the pile
A slow, thick, scarlet streamlet smoked and ran,
Sucked by the sand, but ever rolling down,

The blood of bleating victims. One such lay,
A spotted goat, long-horned, its head bound back
With munja grass; at its stretched throat the knife
Pressed by a priest, who murmured: "This, dread gods,
Of many yajnas cometh as the crown
From Bimbasara: take ye joy to see
The spirted blood, and pleasure in the scent
Of rich flesh roasting 'mid the fragrant flames;
Let the King's sins be laid upon this goat,
And let the fire consume them burning it,
For now I strike."

But Buddha softly said,
"Let him not strike, great King!" and therewith loosed
The victim's bonds, none staying him, so great
His presence was. Then, craving leave, he spake
Of life, which all can take but none can give,
Life, which all creatures love and strive to keep,
Wonderful, dear and pleasant unto each,
Even to the meanest; yea, a boon to all
Where pity is, for pity makes the world
Soft to the weak and noble for the strong.
Unto the dumb lips of his flock he lent
Sad pleading words, showing how man, who prays
For mercy to the gods, is merciless,
Being as god to those; albeit all life
Is linked and kin, and what we slay have given
Meek tribute of the milk and wool, and set
Fast trust upon the hands which murder them.
Also he spake of what the holy books
Do surely teach, how that at death some sink
To bird and beast, and these rise up to man
In wanderings of the spark which grows purged flame.
So were the sacrifice new sin, if so
The fated passage of a soul be stayed.
Nor, spake he, shall one wash his spirit clean

The Light Of Asia

By blood; nor gladden gods, being good, with blood;
Nor bribe them, being evil; nay, nor lay
Upon the brow of innocent bound beasts
One hair's weight of that answer all must give
For all things done amiss or wrongfully,
Alone, each for himself, reckoning with that
The fixed arithmic of the universe,
Which meteth good for good and ill for ill,
Measure for measure, unto deeds, words, thoughts;
Watchful, aware, implacable, unmoved;
Making all futures fruits of all the pasts.
Thus spake he, breathing words so piteous
With such high lordliness of ruth and right,
The priests drew back their garments o'er the hands
Crimsoned with slaughter, and the King came near,
Standing with clasped palms reverencing Buddh;
While still our Lord went on, teaching how fair
This earth were if all living things be linked
In friendliness, and common use of foods
Bloodless and pure; the golden grain, bright fruits,
Sweet herbs which grow for all, the waters wan,
Sufficient drinks and meats. Which when these heard,
The might of gentleness so conquered them,
The priests themselves scattered their altar-flames
And flung away the steel of sacrifice;
And through the land next day passed a decree
Proclaimed by criers, and in this wise graved
On rock and column: "Thus the King's will is:
There hath been slaughter for the sacrifice,
And slaying for the meat, but henceforth none
Shall spill the blood of life nor taste of flesh,
Seeing that knowledge grows, and life is one,
And mercy cometh to the merciful."
So ran the edict, and from those days forth
Sweet peace hath spread between all living kind,
Man and the beasts which serve him, and the birds,

On all those banks of Gunga where our Lord
Taught with his saintly pity and soft speech.

For aye so piteous was the Master's heart
To all that breathe this breath of fleeting life,
Yoked in one fellowship of joys and pains,
That it is written in the holy books
How, in an ancient age--when Buddha wore
A Brahman's form, dwelling upon the rock
Named Munda, by the village of Dalidd--
Drought withered all the land: the young rice died
Ere it could hide a quail; in forest glades
A fierce sun sucked the pools; grasses and herbs
Sickened, and all the woodland creatures fled
Scattering for sustenance. At such a time,
Between the hot walls of a nullah, stretched
On naked stones, our Lord spied, as he passed,
A starving tigress. Hunger in her orbs
Glared with green flame; her dry tongue lolled a span
Beyond the gasping jaws and shrivelled jowl;
Her painted hide hung wrinkled on her ribs,
As when between the rafters sinks a thatch
Rotten with rains; and at the poor lean dugs
Two cubs, whining with famine, tugged and sucked,
Mumbling those milkless teats which rendered nought,
While she, their gaunt dam, licked full motherly
The clamorous twins, yielding her flank to them
With moaning throat, and love stronger than want,
Softening the first of that wild cry wherewith
She laid her famished muzzle to the sand
And roared a savage thunder-peal of woe.
Seeing which bitter strait, and heeding nought
Save the immense compassion of a Buddh,
Our Lord bethought, "There is no other way
To help this murdress of the woods but one.
By sunset these will die, having no meat:

The Light Of Asia

There is no living heart will pity her,
Bloody with ravin, lean for lack of blood.
Lo! if I feed her, who shall lose but I,
And how can love lose doing of its kind
Even to the uttermost?" So saying, Buddh
Silently laid aside sandals and staff,
His sacred thread, turban, and cloth, and came
Forth from behind the milk-bush on the sand,
Saying, "Ho! mother, here is meat for thee!"
Whereat the perishing beast yelped hoarse and shrill,
Sprang from her cubs, and, hurling to the earth
That willing victim, had her feast of him
With all the crooked daggers of her claws
Rending his flesh, and all her yellow fangs
Bathed in his blood: the great cat's burning breath
Mixed with the last sigh of such fearless love.

Thus large the Master's heart was long ago,
Not only now, when with his gracious ruth
He bade cease cruel worship of the gods.
And much King Bimbasara prayed our Lord--
Learning his royal birth and holy search--
To tarry in that city, saying oft
"Thy princely state may not abide such fasts;
Thy hands were made for sceptres, not for alms.
Sojourn with me, who have no son to rule,
And teach my kingdom wisdom, till I die,
Lodged in my palace with a beauteous bride."
But ever spake Siddartha, of set mind
"These things I had, most noble King, and left,
Seeking the Truth; which still I seek, and shall;
Not to be stayed though Sakra's palace ope'd
Its doors of pearl and Devis wooed me in.
I go to build the Kingdom of the Law, journeying to
Gaya and the forest shades,
Where, as I think, the light will come to me;

For nowise here among the Rishis comes
That light, nor from the Shasters, nor from fasts
Borne till the body faints, starved by the soul.
Yet there is light to reach and truth to win;
And surely, O true Friend, if I attain
I will return and quit thy love."

Thereat
Thrice round the Prince King Bimbasara paced,
Reverently bending to the Master's feet,
And bade him speed. So passed our Lord away
Towards Uravilva, not yet comforted,
And wan of face, and weak with six years' quest.
But they upon the hill and in the grove--
Alara, Udra, and the ascetics five--
Had stayed him, saying all was written clear
In holy Shasters, and that none might win
Higher than Sruti and than Smriti--nay,
Not the chief saints!--for how should mortal man
Be wiser than the Jnana-Kand, which tells
How Brahm is bodiless and actionless,
Passionless, calm, unqualified, unchanged,
Pure life, pure thought, pure joy? Or how should man
Its better than the Karmma-Kand, which shows
How he may strip passion and action off,
Break from the bond of self, and so, unsphered,
Be God, and melt into the vast divine,
Flying from false to true, from wars of sense
To peace eternal, where the silence lives?

But the prince heard them, not yet comforted.

The Light Of Asia

Book The Sixth

Thou who wouldst see where dawned the light at last,
North-westwards from the "Thousand Gardens" go
    By Gunga's valley till thy steps be set
On the green hills where those twin streamlets spring
    Nilajan and Mohana; follow them,
    Winding beneath broad-leaved mahua-trees,
    'Mid thickets of the sansar and the bir,
    Till on the plain the shining sisters meet
    In Phalgu's bed, flowing by rocky banks
        To Gaya and the red Barabar hills.
    Hard by that river spreads a thorny waste,
        Uruwelaya named in ancient days,
    With sandhills broken; on its verge a wood
Waves sea-green plumes and tassels 'thwart the sky,
With undergrowth wherethrough a still flood steals,
    Dappled with lotus-blossoms, blue and white,
    And peopled with quick fish and tortoises.
      Near it the village of Senani reared
    Its roofs of grass, nestled amid the palms,
    Peaceful with simple folk and pastoral toils.

      There in the sylvan solitudes once more
    Lord Buddha lived, musing the woes of men,
    The ways of fate, the doctrines of the books,
      The lessons of the creatures of the brake,
    The secrets of the silence whence all come,
      The secrets of the gloom whereto all go,
The life which lies between, like that arch flung
From cloud to cloud across the sky, which hath
      Mists for its masonry and vapoury piers,
      Melting to void again which was so fair
With sapphire hues, garnet, and chrysoprase.
Moon after moon our Lord sate in the wood,
      So meditating these that he forgot

Ofttimes the hour of food, rising from thoughts
Prolonged beyond the sunrise and the noon
To see his bowl unfilled, and eat perforce
Of wild fruit fallen from the boughs o'erhead,
Shaken to earth by chattering ape or plucked
By purple parokeet. Therefore his grace
Faded; his body, worn by stress of soul,
Lost day by day the marks, thirty and two,
Which testify the Buddha. Scarce that leaf,
Fluttering so dry and withered to his feet
From off the sal-branch, bore less likeliness
Of spring's soft greenery than he of him
Who was the princely flower of all his land.

And once at such a time the o'erwrought Prince
Fell to the earth in deadly swoon, all spent,
Even as one slain, who hath no longer breath
Nor any stir of blood; so wan he was,
So motionless. But there came by that way
A shepherd-boy, who saw Siddartha lie
With lids fast-closed, and lines of nameless pain
Fixed on his lips--the fiery noonday sun
Beating upon his head--who, plucking boughs
From wild rose-apple trees, knitted them thick
Into a bower to shade the sacred face.
Also he poured upon the Master's lips
Drops of warm milk, pressed from his she-goat's bag,
Lest, being of low caste, he do wrong to one
So high and holy seeming. But the books
Tell how the jambu-branches, planted thus,
Shot with quick life in wealth of leaf and flower
And glowing fruitage interlaced and close,
So that the bower grew like a tent of silk
Pitched for a king at hunting, decked with studs
Of silver-work and bosses of red gold.
And the boy worshipped, deeming him some God;

The Light Of Asia

But our Lord, gaining breath, arose and asked
Milk in the shepherd's lots. "Ah, my Lord,
I cannot give thee," quoth the lad; "thou seest
I am a Sudra, and my touch defiles!"
Then the World-honoured spake: "Pity and need
Make all flesh kin. There is no caste in blood,
Which runneth of one hue, nor caste in tears,
Which trickle salt with all; neither comes man
To birth with tilka-mark stamped on the brow,
Nor sacred thread on neck. Who doth right deeds
Is twice-born, and who doeth ill deeds vile.
Give me to drink, my brother; when I come
Unto my quest it shall be good for thee."
Thereat the peasant's heart was glad, and gave.

And on another day there passed that road
A band of tinselled, girls, the nautch-dancers
Of Indra's temple in the town, with those
Who made their music--one that beat a drum
Set round with peacock-feathers, one that blew
The piping bansuli, and one that twitched
A three-string sitar. Lightly tripped they down
From ledge to ledge and through the chequered paths
To some gay festival, the silver bells
Chiming soft peals about the small brown feet,
Armlets and wrist-rings tattling answer shrill;
While he that bore the sitar thrummed and twanged
His threads of brass, and she beside him sang--

"Fair goes the dancing when the sitar's tuned;
Tune us the sitar neither low nor high,
And we will dance away the hearts of men.

"The string o'erstretched breaks, and the music flies,
The string o'erslack is dumb, and music dies;
Tune us the sitar neither low nor high."

"So sang the nautch-girl to the pipe and wires,
  Fluttering like some vain, painted butterfly
  From glade to glade along the forest path,
Nor dreamed her light words echoed on the ear
    Of him, that holy man, who sate so rapt
    Under the fig-tree by the path. But Buddh
  Lifted his great brow as the wantons passed,
And spake: 'The foolish ofttimes teach the wise;
    I strain too much this string of life, belike,
    Meaning to make such music as shall save.
  Mine eyes are dim now that they see the truth,
  My strength is waned now that my need is most;
  Would that I had such help as man must have,
  For I shall die, whose life was all men's hope.'"

      Now, by that river dwelt a landholder
      Pious and rich, master of many herds,
    A goodly chief, the friend of all the poor;
  And from his house the village drew its name--
      "Senani." Pleasant and in peace he lived,
        Having for wife Sujata, loveliest
    Of all the dark-eyed daughters of the plain;
      Gentle and true, simple and kind was she,
      Noble of mien, with gracious speech to all
    And gladsome looks--a pearl of womanhood--
      Passing calm years of household happiness
      Beside her lord in that still Indian home,
  Save that no male child blessed their wedded love.
    Wherefore with many prayers she had besought
      Lukshmi, and many nights at full-moon gone
Round the great Lingam, nine times nine, with gifts
      Of rice and jasmine wreaths and sandal oil,
          Praying a boy; also Sujata vowed--
          If this should be--an offering of food
        Unto the Wood-God, plenteous, delicate,

The Light Of Asia

Set in a bowl of gold under his tree,
Such as the lips of Devs may taste and take.
And this had been: for there was born to her
A beauteous boy, now three months old, who lay
Between Sujata's breasts, while she did pace
With grateful footsteps to the Wood-God's shrine,
One arm clasping her crimson sari close
To wrap the babe, that jewel of her joys,
The other lifted high in comely curve
To steady on her head the bowl and dish
Which held the dainty victuals for the God.

But Radha, sent before to sweep the ground
And tie the scarlet threads around the tree,
Came eager, crying, "Ah, dear Mistress! look!
There is the Wood-God sitting in his place,
Revealed, with folded hands upon his knees.
See how the light shines round about his brow!
How mild and great he seems, with heavenly eyes!
Good fortune is it thus to meet the gods."

So,--thinking him divine,--Sujata drew
Tremblingly nigh, and kissed the earth and said,
With sweet face bent: "Would that the Holy One
Inhabiting his grove, Giver of good,
Merciful unto me his handmaiden,
Vouchsafing now his presence, might accept
These our poor gifts of snowy curds, fresh made,
With milk as white as new-carved ivory!"

Therewith into the golden bowl she poured
The curds and milk, and on the hands of Buddh
Dropped attar from a crystal flask-distilled
Out of the hearts of roses; and he ate,
Speaking no word, while the glad mother stood
In reverence apart. But of that meal

So wondrous was the virtue that our Lord
Felt strength and life return as though the nights
Of watching and the days of fast had passed
In dream, as though the spirit with the flesh
Shared that fine meat and plumed its wings anew,
Like some delighted bird at sudden streams
Weary with flight o'er endless wastes of sand,
Which laves the desert dust from neck and crest--
And more Sujata worshipped, seeing our Lord
Grow fairer and his countenance more bright:
"Art thou indeed the God?" she lowly asked,
"And hath my gift found favour?"

But Buddh said, "What is it thou dost bring me?"

"Holy one!"
Answered Sujata, "from our droves I took
Milk of a hundred mothers newly-calved,
And with that milk I fed fifty white cows,
And with their milk twenty-and-five, and then
With theirs twelve more, and yet again with theirs
The six noblest and best of all our herds,
That yield I boiled with sandal and fine spice
In silver lotas, adding rice, well grown
From chosen seed, set in new-broken ground,
So picked that every grain was like a pearl.
This did I of true heart, because I vowed,
Under thy tree, if I should bear a boy
I would make offering for my joy, and now
I have my son and all my life is bliss!"

Softly our Lord drew down the crimson fold,
And, laying on the little head those hands
Which help the world, he said: "Long be thy bliss!
And lightly fall on him the load of life!
For thou hast holpen me who am no God,

The Light Of Asia

But one thy Brother; heretofore a Prince
And now a wanderer, seeking night and day
These six hard years that light which somewhere shines
To lighten all men's darkness, if they knew!
And I shall find the light; yea, now it dawned
Glorious and helpful, when my weak flesh failed
Which this pure food, fair Sister, hath restored,
Drawn manifold through lives to quicken life
As life itself passes by many births
To happier heights and purging off of sins.
Yet dost thou truly find it sweet enough
Only to live? Can life and love suffice?"

Answered Sujata: "Worshipful! my heart
Is little, and a little rain will fill
The lily's cup which hardly moists the field.
It is enough for me to feel life's sun
Shine in my lord's grace and my baby's smile,
Making the loving summer of our home.
Pleasant my days pass filled with household cares
From sunrise when I wake to praise the gods,
And give forth grain, and trim the tulsi-plant,
And set my handmaids to their tasks, till noon
When my lord lays his head upon my lap
Lulled by soft songs and wavings of the fan;
And so to supper-time at quiet eve,
When by his side I stand and serve the cakes.
Then the stars light their silver lamps for sleep,
After the temple and the talk with friends.
How should I not be happy, blest so much,
And bearing him this boy whose tiny hand
Shall lead his soul to Swerga, if it need?
For holy books teach when a man shall plant
Trees for the travelers' shade, and dig a well
For the folks' comfort, and beget a son,
It shall be good for such after their death;

And what the books say, that I humbly take,
Being not wiser than those great of old
Who spake with gods, and knew the hymns and charms,
And all the ways of virtue and of peace.
Also I think that good must come of good
And ill of evil--surely--unto all--
In every place and time--seeing sweet fruit
Groweth from wholesome roots, and bitter things
From poison-stocks; yea, seeing, too, how spite
Breeds hate, and kindness friends, and patience peace
Even while we live; and when 't is willed we die
Shall there not be as good a 'Then' as 'Now'?
Haply much better! since one grain of rice
Shoots a green feather gemmed with fifty pearls,
And all the starry champak's white and gold
Lurks in those little, naked, grey spring-buds.
Ah, Sir! I know there might be woes to bear
Would lay fond Patience with her face in dust;
If this my babe pass first I think my heart
Would break--almost I hope my heart would break!
That I might clasp him dead and wait my lord
In whatsoever world holds faithful wives--
Duteous, attending till his hour should come.
But if Death called Senani, I should mount
The pile and lay that dear head in my lap,
My daily way, rejoicing when the torch
Lit the quick flame and rolled the choking smoke.
For it is written if an Indian wife
Die so, her love shall give her husband's soul
For every hair upon her head a crore
Of years in Swerga. Therefore fear I not.
And therefore, Holy Sir! my life is glad,
Nowise forgetting yet those other lives
Painful and poor, wicked and miserable,
Whereon the gods grant pity! but for me,
What good I see humbly I seek to do,

The Light Of Asia

      And live obedient to the law, in trust
That what will come, and must come, shall come well."

  Then spake our Lord: "Thou teachest them who teach,
      Wiser than wisdom in thy simple lore.
    Be thou content to know not, knowing thus
     Thy way of right and duty: grow, thou flower
 With thy sweet kind in peaceful shade--the light
  Of Truth's high noon is not for tender leaves
 Which must spread broad in other suns and lift
    In later lives a crowned head to the sky.
Thou who hast worshipped me, I worship thee!
    Excellent heart! learned unknowingly,
  As the dove is which flieth home by love.
  In thee is seen why there is hope for man
  And where we hold the wheel of life at will.
 Peace go with thee, and comfort all thy days!
   As thou accomplishest, may I achieve!
He whom thou thoughtest God bids thee wish this."

  "May'st thou achieve," she said, with earnest eyes
Bent on her babe, who reached its tender hands
 To Buddh--knowing, belike, as children know,
More than we deem, and reverencing our Lord;
But he arose--made strong with that pure meat--
And bent his footsteps where a great Tree grew,
  The Bodhi-tree (thenceforward in all years
    Never to fade, and ever to be kept
In homage of the world), beneath whose leaves
It was ordained that Truth should come to Buddh
Which now the Master knew; wherefore he went
  With measured pace, steadfast, majestical,
  Unto the Tree of Wisdom. Oh, ye Worlds!
 Rejoice! our Lord wended unto the Tree!

   Whom--as he passed into its ample shade,

Cloistered with columned dropping stems, and roofed
With vaults of glistening green--the conscious earth
Worshipped with waving grass and sudden flush
Of flowers about his feet. The forest-boughs
Bent down to shade him; from the river sighed
Cool wafts of wind laden with lotus-scents
Breathed by the water-gods. Large wondering eyes
Of woodland creatures--panther, boar, and deer--
At peace that eve, gazed on his face benign
From cave and thicket. From its cold cleft wound
The mottled deadly snake, dancing its hood
In honour of our Lord; bright butterflies
Fluttered their vans, azure and green and gold,
To be his fan-bearers; the fierce kite dropped
Its prey and screamed; the striped palm-squirrel raced
From stem to stem to see; the weaver-bird
Chirped from her swinging nest; the lizard ran;
The koil sang her hymn; the doves flocked round;
Even the creeping things were 'ware and glad.
Voices of earth and air joined in one song,
Which unto ears that hear said: "Lord and Friend!
Lover and Saviour! Thou who hast subdued
Angers and prides, desires and fears and doubts,
Thou that for each and all hast given thyself,
Pass to the Tree! The sad world blesseth thee
Who art the Buddh that shall assuage her woes.
Pass, Hailed and Honoured! strive thy last for us,
King and high Conqueror! thine hour is come;
This is the Night the ages waited for!"

Then fell the night even as our Master sate
Under that Tree. But he who is the Prince
Of Darkness, Mara--knowing this was Buddh
Who should deliver men, and now the hour
When he should find the Truth and save the worlds--
Gave unto all his evil powers command.

The Light Of Asia

Wherefore there trooped from every deepest pit
The fiends who war with Wisdom and the Light,
Arati, Trishna, Raga, and their crew
Of passions, horrors, ignorances, lusts.
The brood of gloom and dread; all hating Buddh,
Seeking to shake his mind; nor knoweth one,
Not even the wisest, how those fiends of Hell
Battled that night to keep the Truth from Buddh:
Sometimes with terrors of the tempest, blasts
Of demon-armies clouding all the wind,
With thunder, and with blinding lightning flung
In jagged javelins of purple wrath
From splitting skies; sometimes with wiles and words
Fair-sounding, 'mid hushed leaves and softened airs
From shapes of witching beauty; wanton songs,
Whispers of love; sometimes with royal allures
Of proffered rule; sometimes with mocking doubts,
Making truth vain. But whether these befell
Without and visible, or whether Buddh
Strove with fell spirits in his inmost heart,
Judge ye:--I write what ancient books have writ.

The ten chief Sins came--Mara's mighty ones,
Angels of evil--Attavada first,
The Sin of Self, who in the Universe
As in a mirror sees her fond face shown,
And crying "I" would have the world say "I,"
And all things perish so if she endure.
"If thou be'st Buddh," she said, "let others grope
Lightless; it is enough that thou art Thou
Changelessly; rise and take the bliss of gods
Who change not, heed not, strive not."
But Buddh spake,
"The right in thee is base, the wrong a curse;
Cheat such as love themselves." Then came wan Doubt,
He that denies--the mocking Sin--and this

Hissed in the Master's ear: "All things are shows,
And vain the knowledge of their vanity;
Thou dost but chase the shadow of thyself;
Rise and go hence, there is no better way
Than patient scorn, nor any help for man,
Nor any staying of his whirling wheel."
But quoth our Lord, "Thou hast no part with me,
False Visikitcha, subtlest of man's foes."
And third came she who gives dark creeds their power,
Silabbat-paramasa, sorceress,
Draped fair in many lands as lowly Faith,
But ever juggling souls with rites and prayers;
The keeper of those keys which lock up Hells
And open Heavens. "Wilt thou dare," she said,
"Put by our sacred books, dethrone our gods,
Unpeople all the temples, shaking down
That law which feeds the priests and props the realms?"
But Buddha answered, "What thou bidd'st me keep
Is form which passes, but the free Truth stands;
Get thee unto thy darkness." Next there drew
Gallantly nigh a braver Tempter, he,
Kama, the King of passions, who hath sway
Over the gods themselves, lord of all loves,
Ruler of Pleasure's realm. Laughing he came
Unto the Tree, bearing his bow of gold
Wreathed with red blooms, and arrows of desire
Pointed with five-tongued delicate flame which stings
The heart it smites sharper than poisoned barb.
And round him came into that lonely place
Bands of bright shapes with heavenly eyes and lips
Singing in lovely words the praise of Love
To music of invisible sweet chords,
So witching, that it seemed the night stood still
To hear them, and the listening stars and moon,
Paused in their orbits while these hymned to Buddh
Of lost delights, and how a mortal man

The Light Of Asia

Findeth nought dearer in the three wide worlds
Than are the yielded loving fragrant breasts
Of Beauty and the rosy breast-blossoms,
Love's rubies; nay, and toucheth nought more high
Than is that dulcet harmony of form
Seen in the lines and charms of loveliness
Unspeakable, yet speaking, soul to soul,
Owned by the bounding blood, worshipped by will
Which leaps to seize it, knowing this is best,
This the true heaven where mortals are like gods,
Makers and Masters, this the gift of gifts
Ever renewed and worth a thousand woes.
For who hath grieved when soft arms shut him safe,
And all life melted to a happy sigh,
And all the world was given in one warm kiss?
So sang, they with soft float of beckoning hands,
Eyes lighted with love-flames, alluring smiles;
In dainty dance their supple sides and limbs
Revealing and concealing like burst buds
Which tell their colour, but hide yet their hearts.
Never so matchless grace delighted eye
As troop by troop these midnight-dancers swept
Nearer the Tree, each daintier than the last,
Murmuring, "O great Siddartha! I am thine,
Taste of my mouth and see if youth is sweet!"
Also, when nothing moved our Master's mind,
Lo! Kama waved his magic bow, and lo!
The band of dancers opened, and a shape
Fairest and stateliest of the throng came forth
Wearing the guise of sweet Yasodhara.
Tender the passion of those dark eyes seemed
Brimming with tears; yearning those outspread arms
Opened towards him; musical that moan
Wherewith the beauteous shadow named his name,
Sighing: "My Prince! I die for lack of thee!
What heaven hast thou found like that we knew

            By bright Rohini in the Pleasure-house,
        Where all these weary years I weep for thee?
            Return, Siddartha! ah, return! But touch
            My lips again, but let me to thy breast
    Once, and these fruitless dreams will end! Ah, look!
        Am I not she thou lovedst?" But Buddh said:
        "For that sweet sake of her thou playest thus
            Fair and false Shadow, is thy playing vain;
        I curse thee not who wear'st a form so dear,
            Yet as thou art, so are all earthly shows.
            Melt to thy void again!" Thereat a cry
    Thrilled through the grove, and all that comely rout
        Faded with flickering wafts of flame, and trail
                Of vaporous ropes.

                    Next under darkening skies
            And noise of rising storm came fiercer Sins
            The rearmost of the Ten, Patigha--Hate--
    With serpents coiled about her waist, which suck
            Poisonous milk from both her hanging dugs,
            And with her curses mix their angry hiss.
            Little wrought she upon that Holy One
    Who with his calm eyes dumbed her bitter lips
    And made her black snakes writhe to hide their fangs.
            Then followed Ruparaga--Lust of days--
        That sensual Sin which out of greed for life
        Forgets to live; and next him Lust of Fame,
            Nobler Aruparaga, she whose spell
    Beguiles the wise, mother of daring deeds,
            Battles and toils. And haughty Mano came,
    The Fiend of Pride; and smooth Self-Righteousness.
        Uddhachcha; and--with many a hideous band
    Of vile and formless things, which crept and flapped
        Toad-like and bat-like--Ignorance, the Dam
        Of Fear and Wrong, Avidya, hideous hag,
    Whose footsteps left the midnight darker, while

The Light Of Asia

The rooted mountains shook, the wild winds howled,
The broken clouds shed from their caverns streams
Of levin-lighted rain; stars shot from heaven,
The solid earth shuddered as if one laid
Flame to her gaping wounds; the torn black air
Was full of whistling wings, of screams and yells,
Of evil faces peering, of vast fronts
Terrible and majestic, Lords of Hell
Who from a thousand Limbos led their troops
To tempt the Master.

But Buddh heeded not,
Sitting serene, with perfect virtue walled
As is a stronghold by its gates and ramps;
Also the Sacred Tree--the Bodhi-tree--
Amid that tumult stirred not, but each leaf
Glistened as still as when on moonlit eves
No zephyr spills the glittering gems of dew;
For all this clamour raged outside the shade
Spread by those cloistered stems.

In the third watch,
The earth being still, the hellish legions fled,
A soft air breathing from the sinking moon,
Our Lord attained samma-sambuddh; he saw
By light which shines beyond our mortal ken
The line of all his lives in all the worlds,
Far back and farther back and farthest yet,
Five hundred lives and fifty. Even as one,
At rest upon a mountain-summit, marks
His path wind up by precipice and crag
Past thick-set woods shrunk to a patch; through bogs
Glittering false-green; down hollows where he toiled
Breathless; on dizzy ridges where his feet
Had well-nigh slipped; beyond the sunny lawns,
The cataract and the cavern and the pool,

Backward to those dim flats wherefrom he sprang
To reach the blue--thus Buddha did behold
Life's upward steps long-linked, from levels low
Where breath is base, to higher slopes and higher
Whereon the ten great Virtues wait to lead
The climber skyward. Also, Buddha saw
How new life reaps what the old life did sow;
How where its march breaks off its march begins;
Holding the gain and answering for the loss;
And how in each life good begets more good,
Evil fresh evil; Death but casting up
Debit or credit, whereupon th' account
In merits or demerits stamps itself
By sure arithmic--where no tittle drops--
Certain and just, on some new-springing life;
Wherein are packed and scored past thoughts and deeds,
Strivings and triumphs, memories and marks
Of lives foregone:

And in the middle watch,
Our Lord attained Abhidjna--insight vast
Ranging beyond this sphere to spheres unnamed,
System on system, countless worlds and suns
Moving in splendid measures, band by band
Linked in division, one yet separate,
The silver islands of a sapphire sea
Shoreless, unfathomed, undiminished, stirred
With waves which roll in restless tides of change.
He saw those Lords of Light who hold their worlds
By bonds invisible, how they themselves
Circle obedient round mightier orbs
Which serve profounder splendours, star to star
Flashing the ceaseless radiance of life
From centres ever shifting unto cirques
Knowing no uttermost. These he beheld
With unsealed vision, and of all those worlds,

The Light Of Asia

Cycle on epicycle, all their tale
Of Kalpas, Mahakalpas--terms of time
Which no man grasps, yea, though he knew to count
The drops in Gunga from her springs to the sea,
Measureless unto speech--whereby these wax
And wane; whereby each of this heavenly host
Fulfils its shining life and darkling dies.
Sakwal by Sakwal, depths and heights be passed
Transported through the blue infinitudes,
Marking--behind all modes, above all spheres,
Beyond the burning impulse of each orb--
That fixed decree at silent work which wills
Evolve the dark to light, the dead to life,
To fulness void, to form the yet unformed,
Good unto better, better unto best,
By wordless edict; having none to bid,
None to forbid; for this is past all gods
Immutable, unspeakable, supreme,
A Power which builds, unbuilds, and builds again,
Ruling all things accordant to the rule
Of virtue, which is beauty, truth, and use.
So that all things do well which serve the Power,
And ill which hinder; nay, the worm does well
Obedient to its kind; the hawk does well
Which carries bleeding quarries to its young;
The dewdrop and the star shine sisterly,
Globing together in the common work;
And man, who lives to die, dies to live well
So if he guide his ways by blamelessness
And earnest will to hinder not but help
All things both great and small which suffer life.
These did our Lord see in the middle watch.

But when the fourth watch came the secret came
Of Sorrow, which with evil mars the law,
As damp and dross hold back the goldsmith's fire.

Then was the Dukha-satya opened him
First of the "Noble Truths"; how Sorrow is
Shadow to life, moving where life doth move;
Not to be laid aside until one lays
Living aside, with all its changing states,
Birth, growth, decay, love, hatred, pleasure, pain,
Being and doing. How that none strips off
These sad delights and pleasant griefs who lacks
Knowledge to know them snares; but he who knows
Avidya--Delusion--sets those snares,
Loves life no longer but ensues escape.
The eyes of such a one are wide; he sees
Delusion breeds Sankhara, Tendency
Perverse: Tendency Energy--Vidnnan--
Whereby comes Namarupa, local form
And name and bodiment, bringing the man
With senses naked to the sensible,
A helpless mirror of all shows which pass
Across his heart; and so Vendana grows--
"Sense-life "--false in its gladness, fell in sadness,
But sad or glad, the Mother of Desire,
Trishna, that thirst which makes the living drink
Deeper and deeper of the false salt waves
Whereon they float--pleasures, ambitions, wealth,
Praise, fame, or domination, conquest, love;
Rich meats and robes, and fair abodes, and pride
Of ancient lines, and lust of days, and strife
To live, and sins that flow from strife, some sweet,
Some bitter. Thus Life's thirst quenches itself
With draughts which double thirst; but who is wise
Tears from his soul this Trishna, feeds his sense
No longer on false shows, fills his firm mind
To seek not, strive not, wrong not; bearing meek
All ills which flow from foregone wrongfulness,
And so constraining passions that they die
Famished; till all the sum of ended life--

The Light Of Asia

The Karma--all that total of a soul
Which is the things it did, the thoughts it had,
The "Self" it wove--with woof of viewless time,
Crossed on the warp invisible of acts--
The outcome of him on the Universe,
Grows pure and sinless; either never more
Needing to find a body and a place,
Or so informing what fresh frame it takes
In new existence that the new toils prove
Lighter and lighter not to be at all,
Thus "finishing the Path"; free from Earth's cheats;
Released from all the skandhas of the flesh;
Broken from ties--from Upandanas--saved
From whirling on the wheel; aroused and sane
As is a man wakened from hateful dreams;
Until--greater than Kings, than Gods more glad!--
The aching craze to live ends, and life glides--
Lifeless--to nameless quiet, nameless joy,
Blessed NIRVANA--sinless, stirless rest
That change which never changes!

Lo! the Dawn
Sprang with Buddh's Victory! lo! in the East
Flamed the first fires of beauteous day, poured forth
Through fleeting folds of Night's black drapery.
High in the widening blue the herald-star
Faded to paler silver as there shot
Brighter and brighter bars of rosy gleam
Across the grey. Far off the shadowy hills
Saw the great Sun, before the world was 'ware,
And donned their crowns of crimson; flower by flower
Felt the warm breath of Morn and 'gan unfold
Their tender lids. Over the spangled grass
Swept the swift footsteps of the lovely Light,
Turning the tears of Night to joyous gems,
Decking the earth with radiance, 'broidering

The sinking storm-clouds with a golden fringe;
Gilding the feathers of the palms, which waved
Glad salutation; darting beams of gold
Into the glades; touching with magic wand
The stream to rippled ruby; in the brake
Finding the mild eyes of the antelopes
And saying, "It is day"; in nested sleep
Touching the small heads under many a wing
And whispering, "Children, praise the light of day!"
Whereat there piped anthems of all the birds!
The koil's fluted song, the bulbul's hymn,
The "morning, morning" of the painted thrush,
The twitter of the sunbirds starting forth
To find the honey ere the bees be out,
The grey crow's caw, the parrot's scream, the strokes
Of the green hammersmith, the myna's chirp,
The never finished love-talk of the doves
Yea! and so holy was the influence
Of that high Dawn which came with victory
That, far and near, in homes of men there spread
An unknown peace. The slayer hid his knife;
The robber laid his plunder back; the shroff
Counted full tale of coins; all evil hearts
Grew gentle, kind hearts gentler, as the balm
Of that divinest Daybreak lightened Earth.
Kings at fierce war called truce; the sick men leaped
Laughing from beds of pain; the dying smiled
As though they knew that happy Morn was sprung
From fountains farther than the utmost East;
And o'er the heart of sad Yasodhara,
Sitting forlorn at Prince Siddartha's bed,
Came sudden bliss, as if love should not fail
Nor such vast sorrow miss to end in joy.
So glad the World was--though it wist not why--
That over desolate wastes went swooning songs
Of mirth, the voice of bodiless Prets and Bhuts

The Light Of Asia

    Foreseeing Buddh; and Devas in the air Cried,
      "It is finished, finished!" and the priests
    Stood with the wondering people in the streets
    Watching those golden splendours flood the sky
    And saying, "There hath happed some mighty thing."
      Also in Ran and jungle grew that day
    Friendship amongst the creatures: spotted deer
    Browsed fearless where the tigress fed her cubs,
    And cheetahs lapped the pool beside the bucks;
    Under the eagle's rock the brown hares scoured
    While his fierce beak but preened an idle wing;
    The snake sunned all his jewels in the beam
    With deadly fangs in sheath; the shrike let pass
    The nestling finch; the emerald halcyons
    Sate dreaming while the fishes played beneath,
    Nor hawked the merops, though the butterflies--
    Crimson and blue and amber-flitted thick
    Around his perch; the Spirit of our Lord
    Lay potent upon man and bird and beast,
    Even while he mused under that Bodhi-tree,
    Glorified with the Conquest gained for all
    And lightened by a Light greater than Day's.

    Then he arose--radiant, rejoicing, strong--
    Beneath the Tree, and lifting high his voice
    Spake this, in hearing of all Times and Worlds:

        Anekajatisangsarang
        Sandhawissang anibhisang
        Gahakarakangawesanto
        Dukkhajatipunappunang.

        Gahakarakadithosi;
        Punagehang nakahasi;
        Sabhatephasukhabhagga,
        Gahakutangwisang Khitang;

Wisangkharagatang chittang,
Janhanangknayamajhaga.

Many a House of Life
Held me--Seeking Ever Him Wrought
These Prisons of the Senses, Sorrow-Fraught;
Sore was My Ceaseless Strife!

But Now,
Thou Builder of this Tabernacle--Thou!
I Know Thee! Never Shalt Thou Build Again
These Walls of Pain,

Nor Raise the Roof-Tree of Deceits, Nor Lay
Fresh Rafters on the Clay:
Broken Thy House is, and the Ridge-Pole Split!
Delusion Fashioned it!
Safe Pass I Thence--Deliverance to Obtain.

Book The Seventh

Sorrowful dwelt the King Suddhodana
All those long years among the Sakya Lords
Lacking the speech and presence of his Son;
Sorrowful sate the sweet Yasodhara
All those long years, knowing no joy of life,
Widowed of him her living Liege and Prince.
And ever, on the news of some recluse
Seen far away by pasturing camel-men
Or traders threading devious paths for gain,
Messengers from the King had gone and come
Bringing account of many a holy sage

The Light Of Asia

Lonely and lost to home; but nought of him
The crown of white Kapilavastu's line,
The glory of her monarch and his hope,
The heart's content of sweet Yasodhara,
Far-wandered now, forgetful, changed, or dead.

But on a day in the Wasanta-time,
When silver sprays swing on the mango-trees
And all the earth is clad with garb of spring,
The Princess sate by that bright garden-stream
Whose gliding glass, bordered with lotus-cups,
Mirrored so often in the bliss gone by
Their clinging hands and meeting lips. Her lids
Were wan with tears, her tender cheeks had thinned;
Her lips' delicious curves were drawn with grief
The lustrous glory of her hair was hid--
Close-bound as widows use; no ornament
She wore, nor any jewel clasped the cloth--
Coarse, and of mourning-white--crossed on her breast.
Slow moved and painfully those small fine feet
Which had the roe's gait and the rose-leaf's fall
In old years at the loving voice of him.
Her eyes, those lamps of love,--which were as if
Sunlight should shine from out the deepest dark,
Illumining Night's peace with Daytime's glow--
Unlighted now, and roving aimlessly,
Scarce marked the clustering signs of coming Spring
So the silk lashes drooped over their orbs.
In one hand was a girdle thick with pearls,
Siddartha's--treasured since that night he fled.
(Ah, bitter Night! mother of weeping days!
When was fond Love so pitiless to love
Save that this scorned to limit love by life?)
The other led her little son, a boy
Divinely fair, the pledge Siddartha left--
Named Rahula--now seven years old, who tripped

Gladsome beside his mother, light of heart
To see the spring-blooms burgeon o'er the world.

So while they lingered by the lotus-pools
And, lightly laughing, Rahula flung rice
To feed the blue and purple fish, and she
With sad eyes watched the swiftly-flying cranes,
Sighing, "O creatures of the wandering wing,
If ye shall light where my dear Lord is hid,
Say that Yasodhara lives nigh to death
For one word of his mouth, one touch of him."--
So, as they played and sighed, mother and child,
Came some among the damsels of the Court
Saying: "Great Princess! there have entered in
At the south gate merchants of Hastinpur
Tripusha called and Bhalluk, men of worth,
Long traveled from the loud sea's edge, who bring
Marvellous lovely webs pictured with gold,
Waved blades of gilded steel, wrought bowls in brass,
Cut ivories, spice, simples, and unknown birds
Treasures of far-off peoples; but they bring
That which doth beggar these, for He is seen!
Thy Lord,--our Lord,--the hope of all the land
Siddartha! they have seen him face to face
Yea, and have worshipped him with knees and brows,
And offered offerings; for he is become
All which was shown, a teacher of the wise,
World-honoured, holy, wonderful; a Buddh
Who doth deliver men and save all flesh
By sweetest speech and pity vast as Heaven
And, lo! he journeyeth hither, these do say."

Then--while the glad blood bounded in her veins
As Gunga leaps when first the mountain snows
Melt at her springs--uprose Yasodhara
And clapped her palms, and laughed, with brimming tears

The Light Of Asia

Beading her lashes. "Oh! call quick," she cried,
"These merchants to my purdah, for mine ears
Thirst like parched throats to drink their blessed news.
Go bring them in,--but if their tale be true,
Say I will fill their girdles with much gold,
With gems that kings shall envy; come ye too,
My girls, for ye shall have guerdon of this
If there be gifts to speak my grateful heart."

So went those merchants to the Pleasure House,
Full softly pacing through its golden ways
With naked feet, amid the peering maids,
Much wondering at the glories of the Court.
Whom, when they came without the purdah's folds,
A voice, tender and eager, filled and charmed
With trembling music, saying: "Ye are come
From far, fair Sirs! and ye have seen my Lord--
Yea, worshipped--for he is become a Buddh,
World-honoured, holy, and delivers men,
And journeyeth hither. Speak! for, if this be,
Friends are ye of my House, welcome and dear."

Then answer made Tripusha: "We have seen
That sacred Master, Princess! we have bowed
Before his feet; for who was lost a Prince
Is found a greater than the King of kings.
Under the Bodhi-tree by Phalgu's bank
That which shall save the world hath late been wrought
By him--the Friend of all, the Prince of all--
Thine most, High Lady! from whose tears men win
The comfort of this Word the Master speaks.
Lo! he is well, as one beyond all ills,
Uplifted as a god from earthly woes,
Shining with risen Truth, golden and clear.
Moreover as he entereth town by town,
Preaching those noble ways which lead to peace,

         The hearts of men follow his path as leaves
            Troop to wind or sheep draw after one
      Who knows the pastures. We ourselves have heard
            By Gaya in the green Tchirnika grove
         Those wondrous lips and done them reverence.
            He cometh hither ere the first rains fall."

         Thus spake he, and Yasodhara, for joy,
       Scarce mastered breath to answer: "Be it well
       Now and at all times with ye, worthy friends,
       Who bring good tidings; but of this great thing
            Wist ye how it befell?"

                Then Bhalluk told
         Such as the people of the valleys knew
      Of that dread night of conflict, when the air
       Darkened with fiendish shadows, and the earth
    Quaked, and the waters swelled with Mara's wrath.
         Also how gloriously that morning broke
         Radiant with rising hopes for man, and how
         The Lord was found rejoicing 'neath his Tree.
         But many days the burden of release--
       To be escaped beyond all storms of doubt,
      Safe on Truth's shore--lay, spake he, on that heart
    A golden load; for how shall men--Buddh mused--
      Who love their sins and cleave to cheats of sense,
         And drink of error from a thousand springs--
         Having no mind to see, nor strength to break
   The fleshly snare which binds them--how should such
            Receive the Twelve Nidanas and the Law
         Redeeming all, yet strange to profit by,
         As the caged bird oft shuns its open door?
            So had we missed the helpful victory
         If, in this earth without a refuge, Buddh
         Winning the way had deemed it all too hard
      For mortal feet, and passed, none following him.

The Light Of Asia

Yet pondered the compassion of our Lord,
But in that hour there rang a voice as sharp
As cry of travail, so as if the earth
Moaned in birth-throe "Nasyami aham bhu
Nasyati loka! Surely I Am Lost,
I And My Creatures:" then a pause, and next
A pleading sigh borne on the western wind,
"Sruyatam dharma, Bhagwat!" Oh, Supreme
Let Thy Great Law Be Uttered! Whereupon
The Master cast his vision forth on flesh,
Saw who should hear and who must wait to hear,
As the keen Sun gilding the lotus-lakes
Seeth which buds will open to his beams
And which are not yet risen from their roots;
Then spake, divinely smiling, "Yea, I preach!
Whoso will listen let him learn the Law."

Afterwards passed he, said they, by the hills
Unto Benares, where he taught the Five,
Showing how birth and death should be destroyed,
And how man hath no fate except past deeds,
No Hell but what he makes, no Heaven too high
For those to reach whose passions sleep subdued.
This was the fifteenth day of Vaishya
Mid-afternoon and that night was full moon.

But, of the Rishis, first Kaundinya
Owned the Four Truths and entered on the Paths;
And after him Bhadraka, Asvajit, Bassav, Mahanama;
also there
Within the Deer-park, at the feet of Buddh,
Yasad the Prince with nobles fifty-four
Hearing the blessed word our Master spake
Worshipped and followed; for there sprang up peace
And knowledge of a new time come for men
In all who heard, as spring the flowers and grass

When water sparkles through a sandy plain.

These sixty--said they--did our Lord send forth,
Made perfect in restraint and passion-free,
To teach the Way; but the World-honoured turned
South from the Deer-park and Isipatan
To Yashti and King Bimbasara's realm,
Where many days he taught; and after these
King Bimbasara and his folk believed,
Learning the law of love and ordered life.
Also he gave the Master, of free gift--
Pouring forth water on the hands of Buddh--
The Bamboo-Garden, named Weluvana,
Wherein are streams and caves and lovely glades;
And the King set a stone there, carved with this:

"Ye dharma hetuppabhawa
Yesan hetun Tathagato;
Aha yesan cha yo nirodho
Ewan wadi Maha samano.

"What life's course and cause sustain
These Tathagato made plain;
What delivers from life's woe
That our Lord hath made us know."

And, in that Garden--said they--there was held
A high Assembly, where the Teacher spake
Wisdom and power, winning all souls which heard,
So that nine hundred took the yellow robe--
Such as the Master wears,--and spread his Law;
And this the gatha was wherewith he closed:

Sabba papassa akaranan;
Kusalassa upasampada;
Sa chitta pariyodapanan;

The Light Of Asia

Etan Budhanusasanan.

"Evil swells the debts to pay,
Good delivers and acquits;
Shun evil, follow good; hold sway
Over thyself. This is the Way."

Whom, when they ended, speaking so of him,
With gifts, and thanks which made the jewels dull,
The Princess recompensed. "But by what road
Wendeth my Lord?" she asked: the merchants said,
"Yojans threescore stretch from the city-walls
To Rajagriha, whence the easy path
Passeth by Sona hither and the hills.
Our oxen, treading eight slow koss a day,
Came in one moon."

Then the King hearing word,
Sent nobles of the Court--well-mounted lords--
Nine separate messengers, each embassy
Bidden to say: "The King Suddhodana--
Nearer the pyre by seven long years of lack,
Wherethrough he hath not ceased to seek for thee--
Prays of his son to come unto his own,
The Throne and people of this longing Realm,
Lest he shall die and see thy face no more."
Also nine horsemen sent Yasodhara
Bidden to say, "The Princess of thy House--
Rahula's mother--craves to see thy face
As the night-blowing moon-flower's swelling heart
Pines for the moon, as pale asoka-buds
Wait for a woman's foot: if thou hast found
More than was lost, she prays her part in this,
Rahula's part, but most of all thyself."
So sped the Sakya Lords, but it befell
That each one, with the message in his mouth,

Entered the Bamboo-Garden in that hour
When Buddha taught his Law; and--hearing--each
Forgot to speak, lost thought of King and quest,
Of the sad Princess even; only gazed
Eye-rapt upon the Master; only hung
Heart-caught upon the speech, compassionate,
Commanding, perfect, pure, enlightening all,
Poured from those sacred lips. Look! like a bee
Winged for the hive, who sees the mogras spread
And scents their utter sweetness on the air,
If he be honey-filled, it matters not;
If night be nigh, or rain, he will not heed;
Needs must he light on those delicious blooms
And drain their nectar; so these messengers
One with another, hearing Buddha's words,
Let go the purpose of their speed, and mixed,
Heedless of all, amid the Master's train.
Wherefore the King bade that Udayi go--
Chiefest in all the Court, and faithfullest,
Siddartha's playmate in the happier days--
Who, as he drew anear the garden, plucked
Blown tufts of tree-wool from the grove and sealed
The entrance of his hearing; thus he came
Safe through the lofty peril of the place
And told the message of the King, and hers.

Then meekly bowed his head and spake our Lord
Before the people: "Surely I shall go!
It is my duty as it was my will;
Let no man miss to render reverence
To those who lend him life, whereby come means
To live and die no more, but safe attain
Blissful Nirvana, if ye keep the Law,
Purging past wrongs and adding nought thereto,
Complete in love and lovely charities.
Let the King know and let the Princess hear

The Light Of Asia

I take the way forthwith." This told, the folk
Of white Kapilavastu and its fields
Made ready for the entrance of their Prince.
At the south gate a bright pavilion rose
With flower-wreathed pillars and the walls of silk
Wrought on their red and green with woven gold.
Also the roads were laid with scented boughs
Of neem and mango, and full mussuks shed
Sandal and jasmine on the dust, and flags
Fluttered; and on the day when he should come
It was ordained how many elephants--
With silver howdahs and their tusks gold-tipped--
Should wait beyond the ford, and where the drums
Should boom "Siddartha cometh!" where the lords
Should light and worship, and the dancing-girls
Where they should strew their flowers with dance and song
So that the steed he rode might tramp knee-deep
In rose and balsam, and the ways be fair;
While the town rang with music and high joy.
This was ordained and all men's ears were pricked
Dawn after dawn to catch the first drum's beat
Announcing, "Now he cometh!"
But it fell Eager to be before--Yasodhara
Rode in her litter to the city-walls
Where soared the bright pavilion. All around
A beauteous garden smiled--Nigrodha named--
Shaded with bel-trees and the green-plumed dates,
New-trimmed and gay with winding walks and banks
Of fruits and flowers; for the southern road
Skirted its lawns, on this hand leaf and bloom,
On that the suburb-huts where base-borns dwelt
Outside the gates, a patient folk and poor,
Whose touch for Kshatriya and priest of Brahm
Were sore defilement. Yet those, too, were quick
With expectation, rising ere the dawn
To peer along the road, to climb the trees

At far-off trumpet of some elephant,
Or stir of temple-drum; and when none came,
Busied with lowly chores to please the Prince;
Sweeping their door-stones, setting forth their flags,
Stringing the fruited fig-leaves into chains,
New furbishing the Lingam, decking new
Yesterday's faded arc of boughs, but aye
Questioning wayfarers if any noise
Be on the road of great Siddartha. These
The Princess marked with lovely languid eyes,
Watching, as they, the southward plain and bent
Like them to listen if the passers gave
News of the path. So fell it she beheld
One slow approaching with his head close shorn,
A yellow cloth over his shoulder cast,
Girt as the hermits are, and in his hand
An earthen bowl, shaped melonwise, the which
Meekly at each hut-door he held a space,
Taking the granted dole with gentle thanks
And all as gently passing where none gave.
Two followed him wearing the yellow robe,
But he who bore the bowl so lordly seemed,
So reverend, and with such a passage moved,
With so commanding presence filled the air,
With such sweet eyes of holiness smote all,
That as they reached him alms the givers gazed
Awestruck upon his face, and some bent down
In worship, and some ran to fetch fresh gifts,
Grieved to be poor; till slowly, group by group,
Children and men and women drew behind
Into his steps, whispering with covered lips,
"Who is he? who? when looked a Rishi thus?"
But as he came with quiet footfall on
Nigh the pavilion, lo! the silken door
Lifted, and, all unveiled, Yasodhara
Stood in his path crying, "Siddartha! Lord!"

The Light Of Asia

With wide eyes streaming and with close-clasped hands,
Then sobbing fell upon his feet, and lay.

Afterwards, when this weeping lady passed
Into the Noble Paths, and one had prayed
Answer from Buddha wherefore-being vowed
Quit of all mortal passion and the touch,
Flower-soft and conquering, of a woman's hands--
He suffered such embrace, the Master said
"The greater beareth with the lesser love
So it may raise it unto easier heights.
Take heed that no man, being 'soaped from bonds,
Vexeth bound souls with boasts of liberty.
Free are ye rather that your freedom spread
By patient winning and sweet wisdom's skill.
Three eras of long toil bring Bodhisats--
Who will be guides and help this darkling world--
Unto deliverance, and the first is named
Of deep 'Resolve,' the second of 'Attempt,'
The third of 'Nomination.' Lo! I lived
In era of Resolve, desiring good,
Searching for wisdom, but mine eyes were sealed.
Count the grey seeds on yonder castor-clump--
So many rains it is since I was Ram,
A merchant of the coast which looketh south
To Lanka and the hiding-place of pearls.
Also in that far time Yasodhara
Dwelt with me in our village by the sea,
Tender as now, and Lukshmi was her name.
And I remember how I journeyed thence
Seeking our gain, for poor the household was
And lowly. Not the less with wistful tears
She prayed me that I should not part, nor tempt
Perils by land and water. 'How could love
Leave what it loved?' she wailed; yet, venturing, I
Passed to the Straits, and after storm and toil

And deadly strife with creatures of the deep,
And woes beneath the midnight and the noon,
Searching the wave I won therefrom a pearl
Moonlike and glorious, such as kings might buy
Emptying their treasury. Then came I glad
Unto mine hills, but over all that land
Famine spread sore; ill was I stead to live
In journey home, and hardly reached my door--
Aching for food--with that white wealth of the sea
Tied in my girdle. Yet no food was there;
And on the threshold she for whom I toiled--
More than myself--lay with her speechless lips
Nigh unto death for one small gift of grain.
Then cried I, 'If there be who hath of grain,
Here is a kingdom's ransom for one life
Give Lukshmi bread and take my moonlight pearl.'
Whereat one brought the last of all his hoard,
Millet--three seers--and clutched the beauteous thing.
But Lukshmi lived and sighed with gathered life,
'Lo! thou didst love indeed!' I spent my pearl
Well in that life to comfort heart and mind
Else quite uncomforted; but these pure pearls,
My last large gain, won from a deeper wave--
The Twelve Nidanas and the Law of Good--
Cannot be spent, nor dimmed, and most fulfil
Their perfect beauty being freeliest given.
For like as is to Meru yonder hill
Heaped by the little ants, and like as dew
Dropped in the footmark of a bounding roe
Unto the shoreless seas, so was that gift
Unto my present giving; and so love--
Vaster in being free from toils of sense--
Was wisest stooping to the weaker heart;
And so the feet of sweet Yasodhara
Passed into peace and bliss, being softly led."

The Light Of Asia

But when the King heard how Siddartha came
Shorn, with the mendicant's sad-coloured cloth,
And stretching out a bowl to gather orts
From base-borns' leavings, wrathful sorrow drove
Love from his heart. Thrice on the ground he spat,
Plucked at his silvered beard, and strode straight forth
Lackeyed by trembling lords. Frowning he clomb
Upon his war-horse, drove the spurs, and dashed,
Angered, through wondering streets and lanes of folk.
Scarce finding breath to say, "The King! bow down!"
Ere the loud cavalcade had clattered by:
Which--at the turning by the Temple-wall
Where the south gate was seen--encountered full
A mighty crowd; to every edge of it
Poured fast more people, till the roads were lost,
Blotted by that huge company which thronged
And grew, close following him whose look serene
Met the old King's. Nor lived the father's wrath
Longer than while the gentle eyes of Buddh
Lingered in worship on his troubled brows,
Then downcast sank, with his true knee, to earth
In proud humility. So dear it seemed
To see the Prince, to know him whole, to mark
That glory greater than of earthly state
Crowning his head, that majesty which brought
All men, so awed and silent, in his steps.
Nathless the King broke forth: "Ends it in this,
That great Siddartha steals into his realm,
Wrapped in a clout, shorn, sandalled, craving food
Of low-borns, he whose life was as a god's,
My son! heir of this spacious power, and heir
Of Kings who did but clap their palms to have
What earth could give or eager service bring?
Thou should'st have come apparelled in thy rank,
With shining spears and tramp of horse and foot.
Lo! all my soldiers camped upon the road,

And all my city waited at the gates;
Where hast thou sojourned through these evil years
Whilst thy crowned father mourned? and she, too, there
Lived as the widows use, foregoing joys;
Never once hearing sound of song or string,
Nor wearing once the festal robe, till now
When in her cloth of gold she welcomes home
A beggar spouse in yellow remnants clad.
Son! why is this?"

"My father!" came reply,
"It is the custom of my race."

"Thy race,"
Answered the King "counteth a hundred thrones
From Maha Sammat, but no deed like this."

"Not of a mortal line," the Master said,
"I spake, but of descent invisible,
The Buddhas who have been and who shall be:
Of these am I, and what they did I do,
And this which now befalls so fell before,
That at his gate a King in warrior-mail
Should meet his son, a Prince in hermit-weeds;
And that, by love and self-control, being more
Than mightiest Kings in all their puissance,
The appointed Helper of the Worlds should bow--
As now do I--and with all lowly love
Proffer, where it is owed for tender debts,
The first-fruits of the treasure he hath brought;
Which now I proffer."

Then the King amazed
Inquired "What treasure?" and the Teacher took
Meekly the royal palm, and while they paced
Through worshipping streets--the Princess and the King

The Light Of Asia

On either side--he told the things which make
For peace and pureness, those Four noble Truths
Which hold all wisdom as shores shut the seas,
Those Eight right Rules whereby who will may walk--
Monarch or slave--upon the perfect Path
That hath its Stages Four and Precepts Eight,
Whereby whoso will live--mighty or mean
Wise or unlearned, man, woman, young or old
Shall soon or late break from the wheels of life,
Attaining blest Nirvana. So they came
Into the Palace-porch, Suddhodana
With brows unknit drinking the mighty words,
And in his own hand carrying Buddha's bowl,
Whilst a new light brightened the lovely eyes
Of sweet Yasodhara and sunned her tears;
And that night entered they the Way of Peace.

Book The Eighth

A broad mead spreads by swift Kohana's bank
At Nagara; five days shall bring a man
In ox-wain thither from Benares' shrines
Eastward and northward journeying. The horns
Of white Himala look upon the place,
Which all the year is glad with blooms and girt
By groves made green from that bright streamlet's wave.
Soft are its slopes and cool its fragrant shades,
And holy all the spirit of the spot
Unto this time: the breath of eve comes hushed
Over the tangled thickets, and high heaps
Of carved red stones cloven by root and stem

Of creeping fig, and clad with waving veil
Of leaf and grass. The still snake glistens forth
From crumbled work of lac and cedar-beams
To coil his folds there on deep-graven slabs;
The lizard dwells and darts o'er painted floors
Where kings have paced; the grey fox litters safe
Under the broken thrones; only the peaks,
And stream, and sloping lawns, and gentle air
Abide unchanged. All else, like all fair shows
Of life, are fled--for this is where it stood,
The city of Suddhodana, the hill
Whereon, upon an eve of gold and blue
At sinking sun Lord Buddha set himself
To teach the Law in hearing of his own.

Lo! ye shall read it in the Sacred Books
How, being met in that glad pleasaunce-place--
A garden in old days with hanging walks,
Fountains, and tanks, and rose-banked terraces
Girdled by gay pavilions and the sweep
Of stately palace-fronts--the Master sate
Eminent, worshipped, all the earnest throng
Catching the opening of his lips to learn
That wisdom which hath made our Asia mild;
Whereto four hundred crores of living souls
Witness this day. Upon the King's right hand
He sate, and round were ranged the Sakya Lords
Ananda, Devadatta--all the Court.
Behind stood Seriyut and Mugallan, chiefs
Of the calm brethren in the yellow garb,
A goodly company. Between his knees
Rahula smiled with wondering childish eyes
Bent on the awful face, while at his feet
Sate sweet Yasodhara, her heartaches gone,
Foreseeing that fair love which doth not feed
On fleeting sense, that life which knows no age,

The Light Of Asia

That blessed last of deaths when Death is dead,
    His victory and hers. Wherefore she laid
    Her hand upon his hands, folding around
    Her silver shoulder-cloth his yellow robe,
    Nearest in all the world to him whose words
    The Three Worlds waited for. I cannot tell
    A small part of the splendid lore which broke
    From Buddha's lips: I am a late-come scribe
    Who love the Master and his love of men,
    And tell this legend, knowing he was wise,
    But have not wit to speak beyond the books;
And time hath blurred their script and ancient sense,
    Which once was new and mighty, moving all.
    A little of that large discourse I know
    Which Buddha spake on the soft Indian eve.
    Also I know it writ that they who heard
Were more--lakhs more--crores more--than could be seen,
    For all the Devas and the Dead thronged there,
    Till Heaven was emptied to the seventh zone
    And uttermost dark Hells opened their bars;
    Also the daylight lingered past its time
    In rose-leaf radiance on the watching peaks,
    So that it seemed night listened in the glens,
    And noon upon the mountains; yea! they write,
The evening stood between them like some maid
Celestial, love-struck, rapt; the smooth-rolled clouds
    Her braided hair; the studded stars the pearls
    And diamonds of her coronal; the moon
    Her forehead jewel, and the deepening dark
Her woven garments. 'T was her close-held breath
    Which came in scented sighs across the lawns
While our Lord taught, and, while he taught, who heard--
    Though he were stranger in the land, or slave,
    High caste or low, come of the Aryan blood,
    Or Mlech or Jungle-dweller--seemed to hear
What tongue his fellows talked. Nay, outside those

Who crowded by the river, great and small,
The birds and beasts and creeping things--'t is writ--
Had sense of Buddha's vast embracing love
And took the promise of his piteous speech;
So that their lives--prisoned in shape of ape,
Tiger, or deer, shagged bear, jackal, or wolf,
Foul-feeding kite, pearled dove, or peacock gemmed,
Squat toad, or speckled serpent, lizard, bat,
Yea, or of fish fanning the river waves--
Touched meekly at the skirts of brotherhood
With man who hath less innocence than these;
And in mute gladness knew their bondage broke
Whilst Buddha spake these things before the King:

Om, Amitaya! measure not with words
Th' Immeasurable; nor sink the string of thought
Into the Fathomless. Who asks doth err,
Who answers, errs. Say nought!

The Books teach Darkness was, at first of all,
And Brahm, sole meditating in that Night;
Look not for Brahm and the Beginning there!
Nor him, nor any light

Shall any gazer see with mortal eyes,
Or any searcher know by mortal mind,
Veil after veil will lift--but there must be
Veil upon veil behind.

Stars sweep and question not. This is enough
That life and death and joy and woe abide;
And cause and sequence, and the course of time,
And Being's ceaseless tide,

Which, ever-changing, runs, linked like a river
By ripples following ripples, fast or slow--

The Light Of Asia

The same yet not the same--from far-off fountain
    To where its waters flow

Into the seas. These, steaming to the Sun,
    Give the lost wavelets back in cloudy fleece
To trickle down the hills, and glide again;
    Having no pause or peace.

This is enough to know, the phantasms are;
The Heavens, Earths, Worlds, and changes changing them
A mighty whirling wheel of strife and stress
    Which none can stay or stem.

Pray not! the Darkness will not brighten!
Ask Nought from the Silence, for it cannot speak!
Vex not your mournful minds with pious pains!
    Ah! Brothers, Sisters! seek

Nought from the helpless gods by gift and hymn,
Nor bribe with blood, nor feed with fruit and cakes;
Within yourselves deliverance must be sought;
    Each man his prison makes.

Each hath such lordship as the loftiest ones;
    Nay, for with Powers above, around, below,
As with all flesh and whatsoever lives,
    Act maketh joy and woe.

What hath been bringeth what shall be, and is,
    Worse--better--last for first and first for last;
The Angels in the Heavens of Gladness reap
    Fruits of a holy past.

The devils in the underworlds wear out
    Deeds that were wicked in an age gone by.
Nothing endures: fair virtues waste with time,

Foul sins grow purged thereby.

Who toiled a slave may come anew a Prince
For gentle worthiness and merit won;
Who ruled a King may wander earth in rags
For things done and undone.

Higher than Indra's ye may lift your lot,
And sink it lower than the worm or gnat;
The end of many myriad lives is this,
The end of myriads that.

Only, while turns this wheel invisible,
No pause, no peace, no staying-place can be;
Who mounts will fall, who falls may mount; the spokes
Go round unceasingly!

If ye lay bound upon the wheel of change,
And no way were of breaking from the chain,
The Heart of boundless Being is a curse,
The Soul of Things fell Pain.

Ye are not bound! the Soul of Things is sweet,
The Heart of Being is celestial rest;
Stronger than woe is will: that which was Good
Doth pass to Better--Best.

I, Buddh, who wept with all my brothers' tears,
Whose heart was broken by a whole world's woe,
Laugh and am glad, for there is Liberty
Ho! ye who suffer! know

Ye suffer from yourselves. None else compels
None other holds you that ye live and die,
And whirl upon the wheel, and hug and kiss

The Light Of Asia

    Its spokes of agony,

Its tire of tears, its nave of nothingness.
Behold, I show you Truth! Lower than hell,
Higher than heaven, outside the utmost stars,
    Farther than Brahm doth dwell,

Before beginning, and without an end,
    As space eternal and as surety sure,
Is fixed a Power divine which moves to good,
    Only its laws endure.

This is its touch upon the blossomed rose,
    The fashion of its hand shaped lotus-leaves;
In dark soil and the silence of the seeds
    The robe of Spring it weaves;

That is its painting on the glorious clouds,
    And these its emeralds on the peacock's train;
It hath its stations in the stars;
    Its slaves in lightning, wind, and rain.

Out of the dark it wrought the heart of man,
Out of dull shells the pheasant's pencilled neck;
    Ever at toil, it brings to loveliness
    All ancient wrath and wreck.

The grey eggs in the golden sun-bird's nest
    Its treasures are, the bees' six-sided cell
Its honey-pot; the ant wots of its ways,
    The white doves know them well.

It spreadeth forth for flight the eagle's wings
What time she beareth home her prey; it sends
The she-wolf to her cubs; for unloved things
    It findeth food and friends.

It is not marred nor stayed in any use,
All liketh it; the sweet white milk it brings
To mothers' breasts; it brings the white drops, too,
Wherewith the young snake stings.

The ordered music of the marching orbs
It makes in viewless canopy of sky;
In deep abyss of earth it hides up gold,
Sards, sapphires, lazuli.

Ever and ever bringing secrets forth,
It sitteth in the green of forest-glades
Nursing strange seedlings at the cedar's root,
Devising leaves, blooms, blades.

It slayeth and it saveth, nowise moved
Except unto the working out of doom;
Its threads are Love and Life; and Death and Pain
The shuttles of its loom.

It maketh and unmaketh, mending all;
What it hath wrought is better than hath been;
Slow grows the splendid pattern that it plans
Its wistful hands between.

This is its work upon the things ye see,
The unseen things are more; men's hearts and minds,
The thoughts of peoples and their ways and wills,
Those, too, the great Law binds.

Unseen it helpeth ye with faithful hands,
Unheard it speaketh stronger than the storm.
Pity and Love are man's because long stress
Moulded blind mass to form.

The Light Of Asia

It will not be contemned of any one;
Who thwarts it loses, and who serves it gains;
The hidden good it pays with peace and bliss,
The hidden ill with pains.
It seeth everywhere and marketh all
Do right--it recompenseth! do one wrong--
The equal retribution must be made,
Though DHARMA tarry long.

It knows not wrath nor pardon; utter-true
Its measures mete, its faultless balance weighs;
Times are as nought, tomorrow it will judge,
Or after many days.

By this the slayer's knife did stab himself;
The unjust judge hath lost his own defender;
The false tongue dooms its lie; the creeping thief
And spoiler rob, to render.

Such is the Law which moves to righteousness,
Which none at last can turn aside or stay;
The heart of it is Love, the end of it
Is Peace and Consummation sweet. Obey!

The Books say well, my Brothers! each man's life
The outcome of his former living is;
The bygone wrongs bring forth sorrows and woes
The bygone right breeds bliss.

That which ye sow ye reap. See yonder fields
The sesamum was sesamum, the corn
Was corn. The Silence and the Darkness knew!
So is a man's fate born.

He cometh, reaper of the things he sowed,

Sesamum, corn, so much cast in past birth;
And so much weed and poison-stuff, which mar
  Him and the aching earth.

If he shall labour rightly, rooting these,
And planting wholesome seedlings where they grew,
Fruitful and fair and clean the ground shall be,
  And rich the harvest due.

If he who liveth, learning whence woe springs,
  Endureth patiently, striving to pay
His utmost debt for ancient evils done
  In Love and Truth alway;

If making none to lack, he throughly purge
The lie and lust of self forth from his blood;
Suffering all meekly, rendering for offence
  Nothing but grace and good;

If he shall day by day dwell merciful,
Holy and just and kind and true; and rend
Desire from where it clings with bleeding roots,
  Till love of life have end:

He--dying--leaveth as the sum of him
A life-count closed, whose ills are dead and quit,
Whose good is quick and mighty, far and near,
  So that fruits follow it.

No need hath such to live as ye name life;
  That which began in him when he began
Is finished: he hath wrought the purpose through
  Of what did make him Man.

Never shall yearnings torture him, nor sins
Stain him, nor ache of earthly joys and woes

The Light Of Asia

Invade his safe eternal peace; nor deaths
And lives recur. He goes

Unto NIRVANA! He is one with life
Yet lives not. He is blest, ceasing to be.
OM, MANI PADME, OM! the Dewdrop slips
Into the shining sea!

This is the doctrine of the KARMA. Learn!
Only when all the dross of sin is quit,
Only when life dies like a white flame spent
Death dies along with it.

Say not "I am," "I was," or "I shall be,"
Think not ye pass from house to house of flesh
Like travelers who remember and forget,
Ill-lodged or well-lodged. Fresh

Issues upon the Universe that sum
Which is the lattermost of lives.
It makes Its habitation as the worm spins silk
And dwells therein. It takes

Function and substance as the snake's egg hatched
Takes scale and fang; as feathered reedseeds fly
O'er rock and loam and sand, until they find
Their marsh and multiply.

Also it issues forth to help or hurt.
When Death the bitter murderer doth smite,
Red roams the unpurged fragment of him, driven
On wings of plague and blight.

But when the mild and just die, sweet airs breathe;
The world grows richer, as if desert-stream

Should sink away to sparkle up again
Purer, with broader gleam.

So merit won winneth the happier age
Which by demerit halteth short of end;
Yet must this Law of Love reign King of all
Before the Kalpas end.

What lets?--Brothers? the Darkness lets! which breeds
Ignorance, mazed whereby ye take these shows
For true, and thirst to have, and, having, cling
To lusts which work you woes.

Ye that will tread the Middle Road, whose course
Bright Reason traces and soft
Quiet smoothes; Ye who will take the high Nirvana-way,
List the Four Noble Truths.

The First Truth is of Sorrow. Be not mocked!
Life which ye prize is long-drawn agony:
Only its pains abide; its pleasures are
As birds which light and fly,

Ache of the birth, ache of the helpless days,
Ache of hot youth and ache of manhood's prime;
Ache of the chill grey years and choking death,
These fill your piteous time.

Sweet is fond Love, but funeral-flames must kiss
The breasts which pillow and the lips which cling;
Gallant is warlike Might, but vultures pick
The joints of chief and King.

Beauteous is Earth, but all its forest-broods
Plot mutual slaughter, hungering to live;
Of sapphire are the skies, but when men cry

The Light Of Asia

Famished, no drops they give.

Ask of the sick, the mourners, ask of him
Who tottereth on his staff, lone and forlorn,
"Liketh thee life?"--these say the babe is wise
That weepeth, being born.

The Second Truth is Sorrow's Cause. What grief
Springs of itself and springs not of Desire?
Senses and things perceived mingle and light
Passion's quick spark of fire:

So flameth Trishna, lust and thirst of things.
Eager ye cleave to shadows, dote on dreams.
A false Self in the midst ye plant, and make
A world around which seems;

Blind to the height beyond, deaf to the sound
Of sweet airs breathed from far past Indra's sky;
Dumb to the summons of the true life kept
For him who false puts by.

So grow the strifes and lusts which make earth's war,
So grieve poor cheated hearts and flow salt tears;
So wag the passions, envies, angers, hates;
So years chase blood-stained years

With wild red feet. So, where the grain should grow,
Spreads the biran-weed with its evil root
And poisonous blossoms; hardly good seeds find
Soil where to fall and shoot;

And drugged with poisonous drink the soul departs,
And fierce with thirst to drink Karma returns;
Sense-struck again the sodden self begins,
And new deceits it earns

The Third is Sorrow's Ceasing. This is peace--
To conquer love of self and lust of life,
To tear deep-rooted passion from the breast,
To still the inward strife;

For love, to clasp Eternal Beauty close;
For glory, to be lord of self; for pleasure,
To live beyond the gods; for countless wealth,
To lay up lasting treasure

Of perfect service rendered, duties done
In charity, soft speech, and stainless days
These riches shall not fade away in life,
Nor any death dispraise.

Then Sorrow ends, for Life and Death have ceased;
How should lamps flicker when their oil is spent?
The old sad count is clear, the new is clean;
Thus hath a man content.

The Fourth Truth is The Way. It openeth wide,
Plain for all feet to tread, easy and near,
The Noble Eightfold Path; it goeth straight
To peace and refuge. Hear!

Manifold tracks lead to yon sister-peaks
Around whose snows the gilded clouds are curled
By steep or gentle slopes the climber comes
Where breaks that other world.

Strong limbs may dare the rugged road which storms,
Soaring and perilous, the mountain's breast;
The weak must wind from slower ledge to ledge
With many a place of rest.

The Light Of Asia

So is the Eightfold Path which brings to peace;
By lower or by upper heights it goes.
The firm soul hastes, the feeble tarries. All
Will reach the sunlit snows.

The First good Level is Right Doctrine.
Walk In fear of Dharma, shunning all offence;
In heed of Karma, which doth make man's fate;
In lordship over sense.

The Second is Right Purpose. Have good-will
To all that lives, letting unkindness die
And greed and wrath; so that your lives be made
Like soft airs passing by.

The Third is Right Discourse. Govern the lips
As they were palace-doors, the King within;
Tranquil and fair and courteous be all words
Which from that presence win.

The Fourth is Right Behavior. Let each act
Assoil a fault or help a merit grow;
Like threads of silver seen through crystal beads
Let love through good deeds show.

Four higher roadways be. Only those feet
May tread them which have done with earthly things--
Right Purity, Right Thought, Right Loneliness,
Right Rapture. Spread no wings

For sunward flight, thou soul with unplumed vans
Sweet is the lower air and safe, and known
The homely levels: only strong ones leave
The nest each makes his own.

Dear is the love, I know, of Wife and Child;
Pleasant the friends and pastimes of your years;
Fruitful of good Life's gentle charities;
False, though firm-set, its fears.
Live--ye who must--such lives as live on these;
Make golden stair-ways of your weakness; rise
By daily sojourn with those phantasies
To lovelier verities.

So shall ye pass to clearer heights and find
Easier ascents and lighter loads of sins,
And larger will to burst the bonds of sense,
Entering the Path. Who wins

To such commencement hath the First Stage touched;
He knows the Noble Truths, the Eightfold Road;
By few or many steps such shall attain
NIRVANA's blest abode.

Who standeth at the Second Stage, made free
From doubts, delusions, and the inward strife,
Lord of all lusts, quit of the priests and books,
Shall live but one more life.

Yet onward lies the Third Stage: purged and pure
Hath grown the stately spirit here, hath risen
To love all living things in perfect peace.
His life at end, life's prison

Is broken. Nay, there are who surely pass
Living and visible to utmost goal
By Fourth Stage of the Holy ones--the Buddhs--
And they of stainless soul.

Lo! like fierce foes slain by some warrior,
Ten sins along these Stages lie in dust,

The Light Of Asia

The Love of Self, False Faith, and Doubt are three,
    Two more, Hatred and Lust.

Who of these Five is conqueror hath trod
    Three stages out of Four: yet there abide
The Love of Life on earth, Desire for Heaven,
    Self-Praise, Error, and Pride.

As one who stands on yonder snowy horn
Having nought o'er him but the boundless blue,
So, these sins being slain, the man is come
    NIRVANA's verge unto.

Him the Gods envy from their lower seats;
Him the Three Worlds in ruin should not shake;
All life is lived for him, all deaths are dead;
    Karma will no more make

New houses. Seeking nothing, he gains all;
    Foregoing self, the Universe grows "I":
If any teach NIRVANA is to cease,
    Say unto such they lie.

If any teach NIRVANA is to live,
    Say unto such they err; not knowing this,
Nor what light shines beyond their broken lamps,
    Nor lifeless, timeless bliss.

Enter the Path! There is no grief like Hate!
    No pains like passions, no deceit like sense!
Enter the Path! far hath he gone whose foot
    Treads down one fond offence.

Enter the Path! There spring the healing streams
Quenching all thirst! there bloom th' immortal flowers
Carpeting all the way with joy! there throng,

Swiftest and sweetest hours!

More is the treasure of the Law than gems;
Sweeter than comb its sweetness; its delights
Delightful past compare. Thereby to live
    Hear the Five Rules aright:--

Kill not--for Pity's sake--and lest ye slay
The meanest thing upon its upward way.

Give freely and receive, but take from none
By greed, or force, or fraud, what is his own.

Bear not false witness, slander not, nor lie;
Truth is the speech of inward purity.

Shun drugs and drinks which work the wit abuse;
Clear minds, clean bodies, need no soma juice.

Touch not thy neighbour's wife, neither commit
Sins of the flesh unlawful and unfit.

These words the Master spake of duties due
To father, mother, children, fellows, friends;
Teaching how such as may not swiftly break
The clinging chains of sense--whose feet are weak
    To tread the higher road--should order so
    This life of flesh that all their hither days
    Pass blameless in discharge of charities
And first true footfalls in the Eightfold Path;
    Living pure, reverent, patient, pitiful,
Loving all things which live even as themselves;
    Because what falls for ill is fruit of ill
Wrought in the past, and what falls well of good;
    And that by howsomuch the householder
Purgeth himself of self and helps the world,

The Light Of Asia

By so much happier comes he to next stage,
In so much bettered being. This he spake,
As also long before, when our Lord walked
By Rajagriha in the Bamboo-Grove
For on a dawn he walked there and beheld
The householder Singala, newly bathed,
Bowing himself with bare head to the earth,
To Heaven, and all four quarters; while he threw
Rice, red and white, from both hands. "Wherefore thus
Bowest thou, Brother?" said the Lord; and he,
"It is the way, Great Sir! our fathers taught
At every dawn, before the toil begins,
To hold off evil from the sky above
And earth beneath, and all the winds which blow."
Then the World-honoured spake: "Scatter not rice,
But offer loving thoughts and acts to all.
To parents as the East where rises light;
To teachers as the South whence rich gifts come;
To wife and children as the West where gleam
Colours of love and calm, and all days end;
To friends and kinsmen and all men as North;
To humblest living things beneath, to Saints
And Angels and the blessed Dead above
So shall all evil be shut off, and so
The six main quarters will be safely kept."

But to his own, them of the yellow robe
They who, as wakened eagles, soar with scorn
From life's low vale, and wing towards the Sun
To these he taught the Ten Observances
The Dasa-Sil, and how a mendicant
Must know the Three Doors and the Triple Thoughts;
The Sixfold States of Mind; the Fivefold Powers;
The Eight High Gates of Purity; the Modes
Of Understanding; Iddhi; Upeksha;
The Five Great Meditations, which are food

Sweeter than Amrit for the holy soul;
The Jhana's and the Three Chief Refuges.
Also he taught his own how they should dwell;
How live, free from the snares of love and wealth;
What eat and drink and carry--three plain cloths,
Yellow, of stitched stuff, worn with shoulder bare
A girdle, almsbowl, strainer. Thus he laid
The great foundations of our Sangha well,
That noble Order of the Yellow Robe
Which to this day standeth to help the World.

So all that night he spake, teaching the Law
And on no eyes fell sleep--for they who heard
Rejoiced with tireless joy. Also the King,
When this was finished, rose upon his throne
And with bared feet bowed low before his Son
Kissing his hem; and said, "Take me, O Son!
Lowest and least of all thy Company."
And sweet Yasodhara, all happy now,--
Cried "Give to Rahula--thou Blessed One!
The Treasure of the Kingdom of thy Word
For his inheritance." Thus passed these Three
Into the Path.

Here endeth what I write
Who love the Master for his love of us,
A little knowing, little have I told
Touching the Teacher and the Ways of Peace.
Forty-five rains thereafter showed he those
In many lands and many tongues and gave
Our Asia light, that still is beautiful,
Conquering the world with spirit of strong grace
All which is written in the holy Books,
And where he passed and what proud Emperors
Carved his sweet words upon the rocks and caves:
And how--in fulness of the times--it fell

The Light Of Asia

The Buddha died, the great Tathagato,
Even as a man 'mongst men, fulfilling all
And how a thousand thousand crores since then
Have trod the Path which leads whither he went
Unto NIRVANA where the Silence lives.

Ah! Blessed Lord! Oh, High Deliverer!
Forgive this feeble script, which doth thee wrong.
Measuring with little wit thy lofty love.
Ah! Lover! Brother! Guide! Lamp of the law!
I take my refuge in they name and thee!
I take my refuge in they order! OM!
The dew is on the lotus!--Rise, Great Sun!
And lift my leaf and mix me with the wave.
Om Mani Padme Hum, the sunrise comes!
The Dewdrop Slips Into The Shining Sea!

The End

www.ingramcontent.com/pod-product-compliance
Lightning Source LLC
Chambersburg PA
CBHW062204080426
42734CB00010B/1783